RECIPES *from* MY HOME KITCHEN

CHRISTINE HA

RECIPES

from **MY**

HOME

KITCHEN

Asian and American
Comfort Food
from the Winner of
MasterChef Season 3

RODALE.

Rodale books may be purchased for business or promotional use or for special sales.
For information, please write to:
Special Markets Department, Rodale Inc., 733 Third Avenue, New York, NY 10017

Printed in the United States of America
Rodale Inc. makes every effort to use acid-free ♾, recycled paper ♻.

Photographs by Mitch Mandel/Rodale Images

Book design by Christina Gaugler

Library of Congress Cataloging-in-Publication Data is on file with the publisher

ISBN 978-1-62336-094-8 hardcover

Distributed to the trade by Macmillan

2 4 6 8 10 9 7 5 3 1 hardcover

We inspire and enable people to improve their lives and the world around them.
rodalebooks.com

For my parents, especially my mother,
who lives on through me and these recipes.

Contents

Foreword

Christine Ha walked into my life with a white cane and a brilliant dish on the first day of the third season of my FOX show, *MasterChef*. She was competing with 99 other home cooks for a coveted white apron and a place in the *MasterChef* kitchen . . . and she was *blind*. I thought I'd seen everything in my 20-odd years in the culinary industry and 3 years as host of this globally captivating TV cooking competition for amateurs. But a blind contestant? All sorts of questions were running through my head. How would she handle hot stoves? What about sharp knives? Would she chop off her fingers?

But that first dish Christine made for us—Clay Pot Catfish with Quick Pickled Cucumbers and Carrots—was both unbelievable and unforgettable. It had a depth of flavor that tasted as though it had been cooking for hours, though Christine had created the dish from scratch in just 60 minutes. I was pretty intrigued and impressed that this dish had been made by an amateur, let alone someone without the ability to see what she was creating. It was unimaginable to me. It was clear that this was a woman who was using each of her other senses—touch, hearing, taste, and smell—to elevate her cooking to an extraordinary level. I was really excited. I also felt immediately that, in Christine, we had a young woman whose unique story and life experience could be a powerful and inspiring tool to help others achieve their dreams. While there were often doubtful voices around me, I had faith that Christine's blindness could, in a very strange way, almost be an advantage.

I am very pleased to say that I was right! Christine went on to eliminate each and every contender and nail the title of MasterChef USA. Her dishes just kept getting better and better. Her signature Asian-influenced comfort-food appetizers, entrées, and desserts demonstrate an innate connection to flavor and texture that I rarely experience in professional chefs, let alone amateur cooks. An equally talented writer, Christine's dishes immediately whisk you off into her imagination. She embodies the essence of what it takes to become a great cookery writer.

In the short amount of time since Christine's taken the *MasterChef* crown, she's gone on to judge *MasterChef Vietnam* and inspire thousands of people around the world with her against-all-odds story, brilliant cooking demonstrations, and motivational speeches. She's also turned in her master's thesis in creative writing at the University of Houston and, now this, her first cookbook.

I love Asian food. I've enjoyed some of the best dishes of my life during my trips to Asia. But I know that these foreign flavors can often be intimidating to others who don't have that heritage or experience of traveling in the Far East. But have no fear. Christine has taken those flavors by her Texan bullhorns and created a huge array of delicious dishes with both Asian and Southern influences and turned them into simple recipes perfectly suited to the modern home cook.

I hope that you enjoy taking inspiration from Christine's phenomenal first book. I've had the great fortune of tasting many of her dishes. Now it's your turn.

—*Gordon Ramsay*

Introduction

I did not grow up cooking by my mama's side. I am not one of those people who can say I've always loved food and have been cooking since I was old enough to hold a spoon. Quite the opposite, actually. My aunts and uncles tell stories of how, as a child, I used to be an extremely picky eater, taking hours to eat a bowl of rice, often turning it into porridge with my tears. My mama forbade my leaving the table until every grain of rice was gone. One time, I snuck away and flushed my food down the toilet. "You didn't eat all that food in 10 seconds," she said. My mama was no fool.

I left for college with only three recipes in my culinary repertoire: scrambled eggs with toast, frozen pizza, and instant ramen. When I moved out of the dorms and into an apartment next to campus, I was suddenly without the convenience of a cafeteria meal plan. Instead, I found myself standing in the middle of a 5-by-4-foot linoleum-floored kitchenette with faded Formica counters and a cracked ceramic sink. I purchased my first set of knives and cookware for less than 50 dollars. Then I went to a secondhand bookstore and bought an Asian recipe book.

I first tried to make a noodle soup in which the dumplings broke and the broth became cloudy with starch. My roommates pursed their lips and shook their heads, leaving me to eat my murky meal alone. My next cooking experiment was ginger braised chicken. The tantalizing aromas of onion, ginger, and fish sauce filled our cozy apartment. This time, my friends were more than eager to trust my cooking and even asked for seconds. The notion that I could create something that evoked joy in others was deeply fulfilling, and this became the impetus for my desire to master all things culinary. It is a lifelong journey, and I still learn something new in the kitchen every day.

Unfortunately, when I began my love affair with the culinary arts, I struggled with an equally disheartening diagnosis of neuromyelitis optica (NMO) and subsequent vision loss. I recall being home alone one afternoon in 2007, shortly after my vision had worsened to the level it is today. It felt as though I were floating through a continuous fog. I was hungry and so made my way to the kitchen by feeling along the walls. I retrieved what I knew to be peanut butter and jelly but had trouble spreading them onto the bread. Globs of strawberry preserves covered the counter, and only one corner of the sandwich was covered with a clump of peanut butter. In putting together the sandwich, I misaligned the slices and ended up with jelly dripping down my arm. I remember being so upset with myself and my incapability that I just tossed the whole thing into the trash and cried.

Only a few years earlier, I was preparing the entire Thanksgiving dinner for my family. And now, I had trouble making a simple peanut butter and jelly sandwich. I thought I might have to give up cooking forever, and this broke my heart.

With the encouragement and support of friends and rehabilitation counselors, however, I eventually gained the determination and adaptive tools to cook again. I relearned how to use a knife with more precision and care. A talking thermometer, a beeping liquid measurer, extra-long fire-retardant oven mitts, and other tools helped me make my way around the kitchen safely again. Perhaps most importantly, I learned to rely on my other senses in preparing food. It took months, maybe even years, for me to relearn how to cook an entire meal, but when I think back to the peanut butter and jelly sandwich I'd muddled 6 years ago, I am reminded of how far I've come.

Food, like love, is a basic human need. Everyone needs sustenance to survive. Food can unite people regardless of culture, ethnicity, religion, political ideals, or socioeconomic backgrounds. Two people who may not speak the same language can sit down to a meal together and thereby instantly have something in common: the desire to partake.

One of my favorite things to do is travel and immerse myself in another region or country's culture; it helps remind me just how big the world is and gain a perspective as to my place in it. Since I lost my vision, sightseeing has naturally become quite boring for me. Instead, the way I experience another place and people is through food. Whether it's the catch of the day made into nigiri in Tokyo, hot baguettes from a Paris boulangerie, ceviche from a cafe in Cabo, or beef brisket from Texas hill country, I love to do as the locals do and eat what the locals eat. This is how I make a connection with them and is ultimately why I cook: to connect with others.

I learned all about connecting from my parents, who came to the United States as refugees in 1975. While my mama primarily cooked Vietnamese food in our house, our home was in America, and I grew up eating both cuisines. My mama was the best cook I knew (and I don't say this just because she's my mama). The intoxicating aromas of her noodle soups and braised meats would call me out of bed every Saturday morning. I was fortunate to eat well at home in my youth, but as children often do, I took it for granted. When my mama died 5 days before my 14th birthday, her food became forever lost. She left behind no written recipes, save for a fragmented list of ingredients for her *phở bò*. Mysteriously, even that list has disappeared.

My desire to pull together the recipes that comfort me is rooted in my nostalgia for that time in my life when my mama was alive. These foods are not fancy, don't require extensive knowledge of technique, and usually don't call for expensive ingredients. What they do require is cooking from the heart. That's what I did when I was a contestant on *MasterChef* Season 3. I prepared food straight from my heart—clay pot catfish, buttermilk fried chicken, braised pork belly with egg—and looked to the foods that soothed me from the time I was a little girl in my mama's kitchen to the later years of my life, when I was on my own. When *MasterChef* Season 3 judge Gordon Ramsay asked me which prize I longed for the most—the trophy, the cookbook, or the money—I answered without a doubt that it was the cookbook. "I want to share myself with the world," I told him.

By re-creating these recipes and reading the stories behind them, I hope you feel like I am right there cooking and communing with you in your own kitchen, the way I imagine my own mama next to me in mine.

Happy cooking, and always remember to cook from your heart.

xoxo

Christine Ha

Houston, 2013

Chapter 1

Snacks and Starters

Appetizers and small plates are often my favorite things to eat. When hunger kicks in, they're the perfect way to whet the appetite without killing it. In fact, the best snacks and starters not only leave room for the main course but set the tone for the entire meal. They need to wow the diner in both appearance and, of course, taste. This doesn't always translate to fancy food. On the contrary, some of the most successful snacks and appetizers I've served are just the opposite. Consider classic tomato bruschetta. It's not new, but it never stops delighting, especially when it's made in season with tomatoes and sweet basil straight from the garden. Kale chips, among the easiest snacks to make, require no plates or utensils to eat but are served in a big communal bowl and eaten by hand. I have also included here a few recipes that are great to serve your mother-in-law, the boss, or anyone you're trying to impress. Salmon Poke, a no-cook preparation of glistening salmon tossed in sesame oil, is easy to put together, but the tiny mound of shiny jewels looks quite special. Sweetbreads, too, are here, a good choice when you're entertaining more formally. As with all my cooking, you'll find a little bit of the West and a little bit of the East in this chapter. In some cases, I've taken an American classic and given it a Southeast Asian twist. Caramelized Chicken Wings, for example, are marinated in garlic and fish sauce (some of my favorite ingredients). Whatever the iteration, pizza or flatbread, candied bacon or seaweed rice rolls, I am lucky to hail from such disparate places when it comes to food; it makes for an interesting way to start a meal.

CLASSIC BRUSCHETTA

✧ **When I backpacked through western Europe** the summer after I graduated from college, the country I most anticipated visiting was Italy. Growing up on pizzas and spaghetti, my naive 22-year-old self thought as soon as I stepped off the train in Rome, I'd be surrounded by pies and pastas galore. Unfortunately, I came to learn a few vital lessons the hard way: (1) One couldn't get very far on a backpacker's budget of a few lire per day, and (2) every place I could afford served chicken and potatoes only.

Of all the foods I ate in Rome, the most memorable was a simple plate of bruschetta served to me by a gentle waiter at an open-air café. I had no idea what bruschetta was at the time, but I ordered it because it was one of the cheaper items on the menu. With ripe, sweet tomatoes and fragrant basil, the bruschetta turned out to be the best thing I ate during my stay. I adored how something so simple could taste so indulgent, especially with a glass of red table wine. Sitting there, I no longer felt like a backpacker on a budget. Nowadays whenever I want to re-create that sweet memory of romantic Rome, I prepare this dish. *Buon appetito!*

SERVES 6

2 Roma tomatoes, diced and strained

¼ red onion, diced

6 fresh basil leaves, thinly sliced, plus additional for garnish

Kosher salt and freshly ground black pepper

1 tablespoon extra-virgin olive oil

4 teaspoons balsamic vinegar

1½ tablespoons butter, melted

1 French baguette, cut into ¾-inch-thick slices

⅛ cup (½ ounce) grated Parmesan

Preheat the oven to 350°F.

In a medium bowl, combine the tomatoes, onion, 6 fresh basil leaves, salt, and pepper. Add the olive oil and balsamic vinegar and toss to coat thoroughly. Set aside for at least 30 minutes.

Brush the butter onto both sides of each bread slice and place on a baking sheet. Bake until the bread is light golden, 2 to 3 minutes per side. Spoon the tomato mixture on top of each slice and dust with the Parmesan. Garnish with the additional basil leaves and serve.

THE PICK FOR POTLUCKS

Bruschetta is my go-to recipe for potlucks or parties when I'm short on time but want to show up with something that looks like it took a lot of effort to prepare. Just be sure to keep the tomato-basil mixture separate from the slices of toast until it's time to serve, or you'll suffer from soggy bread syndrome—not good.

KALE AND MUSHROOM CHIPS

✧ **Who doesn't love a good chip?** From the ages of 6 to 11, the only things sustaining me during summer breaks were potato chips. My favorite flavor was sour cream and onion, and I could polish off a family-sized bag over the course of a day. Sick, I know.

Today, I am still obsessed with chips. But now that I'm older (and a tad wiser), I know all those starchy potatoes can't be good for me. Instead, I turn to kale and maitake mushrooms, both of which pack major health benefits. I created this recipe for the finale of *MasterChef* Season 3 and served it with some pickled shallots as an accompaniment to my Braised Pork Belly with Egg (page 65). But the best way to eat these chips, in my opinion, is straight from the paper towel–lined plate.

SERVES 4

Canola oil

8 ounces maitake, oyster, or shiitake mushrooms, brushed clean and stems removed

2 tablespoons quick-mixing flour such as Wondra

2 large bunches kale, stems removed and coarsely chopped

Fleur de sel or Maldon sea salt

Fill a deep pot with 3 inches of oil and heat over high heat until hot.

Meanwhile, in a large bowl, combine the mushrooms with the flour and toss to coat. Shake to remove excess flour.

Working in batches, deep-fry the mushrooms until golden and crispy, 30 to 45 seconds. Using a slotted spoon, transfer the mushrooms to a paper towel–lined platter to drain.

When the oil returns to high heat, deep-fry the kale in batches until crispy, 10 to 15 seconds. Using a slotted spoon, transfer the kale to a paper towel–lined platter to drain.

In a serving bowl, combine the kale and mushrooms, sprinkle them with the salt, and gently toss. Serve immediately.

YOU GET OUT OF IT WHAT YOU PUT INTO IT

With just five ingredients here, it's essential to use the very best you can find. Using a special salt may seem frivolous, but there's a reason I suggest it: You want the salt to enhance the flavors of the vegetables and quickly melt away on your tongue, an experience you won't get from, say, iodized table salt from a canister. So forgo Starbucks a couple of times and use that money instead to buy a small stash of fancy salt.

PROSCIUTTO AND ARUGULA PIZZA

When I was a child, my parents often used pizza to bribe me. "If you finish all your homework early, we'll order pizza for dinner." Or "If you're a good girl while Mommy shops for 6 hours, you'll get some pizza." Or "If you don't cry in ice-skating class today, you'll get pizza for lunch." Pizza was a constant reward throughout my childhood, so it's no wonder I love it so much. I may as well call it Pavlovian pie.

A good pizza is all about the crust. It should be crispy with a perfect balance of sugar, salt, and yeast. I love a simple pie; toppings shouldn't be overdone to the point where the crust sags when you pick up a slice with your hands.

During a recent trip to San Francisco, I had a Neapolitan pizza topped with fresh mozzarella, prosciutto, and arugula. It was love at first taste. Once home, I found myself dreaming about that pizza so much that I went to work in the kitchen. While my version isn't a true Neapolitan pie (for one, it utilizes a rolling pin, and that's just the beginning), it marries the best of both worlds: the prosciutto, arugula, and mozzarella from the classic, with a crust and sauce similar to those I grew up eating. It has become a household favorite, especially for weekend movie nights. It's so good that you'll be able to bribe everyone into watching that vampire love/Vin Diesel film you've been dying to see. (You know who you are.)

MAKES ONE 10-INCH PIZZA (SERVES 4 TO 6)

1¼ cups all-purpose flour plus extra for dusting

1 tablespoon sugar

1 teaspoon active dry yeast

½ teaspoon kosher salt

¼ teaspoon dried basil

½ cup flat beer, preferably lager

1 tablespoon butter, softened

1 tablespoon olive oil

2 teaspoons cornmeal

½ cup No-Cook Pizza Sauce (page 176)

½ cup (2 ounces) fresh mozzarella cheese, thinly sliced

3 slices prosciutto, coarsely chopped

½ cup arugula

In the bowl of a stand mixer fitted with a dough hook, combine the flour, sugar, yeast, salt, basil, beer, and butter. Mix on low speed until the dough comes together. Increase the speed to medium and continue mixing until a ball forms around the hook. If the dough is very dry, add a dash of beer; if it is too wet, add a pinch of flour. The dough should be slightly tacky. Once the dough forms a ball, increase the speed to medium-high and knead for 6 minutes.

Coat the inside of a large bowl with $1\frac{1}{2}$ teaspoons of the olive oil. Transfer the dough to the bowl and cover it with a damp towel. Set aside to rise in a warm, draft-free area until the dough has doubled in size, 1 hour to 1 hour 15 minutes.

Place a pizza stone on a rack in the lower third of the oven. Preheat the oven to 400°F. Dust a clean work surface and a rolling pin with flour. Roll out the pizza dough into a 10-inch circle approximately $\frac{1}{8}$ inch thick.

Sprinkle the cornmeal onto the pizza stone. Carefully lift the dough onto a pizza peel and brush it with the remaining $1\frac{1}{2}$ teaspoons olive oil. Bake for 10 minutes. Using the peel, remove the dough from the oven and spread the sauce evenly over it. Arrange the mozzarella on top and bake until the cheese is melted and the crust is light gold and crispy, 10 to 15 minutes. Remove from the oven with the peel and top with the prosciutto and arugula. Cut into wedges and serve immediately.

"KNEAD" TO WORK OUT?

If you're looking to build your triceps, you can forgo the stand mixer and knead the dough with your hands. Combine the ingredients as above and work them with your hands until they come together. Turn the dough out onto a floured work surface and, with lightly floured hands, begin kneading: Using the heels of your hands, press down into the center of the ball of dough; fold the bottom half of the dough up over the center; turn the dough a quarter turn; repeat. Do this for 10 to 15 minutes as quickly as possible. You know you're finished when you have one pretty ball of smooth dough— and two sore arms.

TIME-SAVING TIP

The dough can be made the day before and, in my opinion, tastes even better when it is. After you let it rise, cover and refrigerate it overnight. Remove the dough from the refrigerator and let it sit for about 2 hours to warm up to room temperature before rolling it out. Want to save even more time? Use a good-quality canned pizza sauce instead of making it from scratch.

BOMBAY FLATBREAD

✧ **I whipped up this flatbread** during a pizza stone challenge for *MasterChef* Season 3. The inspiration comes from a pizza joint in my hometown of Houston where you can get cilantro mint chutney and *saag paneer* (a creamy concoction made of spinach and cheese) on your pie. I finished off my flatbread by topping it with a fried egg because, in my opinion, few things in life aren't made better with eggs. Before eating, break the yolk and let it run all over; the egg adds dimension to the flatbread—so much for it being "flat." It's the cherry—er, egg—on top!

MAKES 4

FOR THE BREAD

2¾ cups all-purpose flour

1 teaspoon kosher salt

1 teaspoon sugar

2 tablespoons olive oil

1 cup beer, chilled

FOR THE CHICKEN

1 teaspoon peeled, minced fresh ginger

1 clove garlic, minced

1 teaspoon kosher salt

¼ teaspoon curry powder

¼ teaspoon garam masala

¼ teaspoon turmeric

12 ounces boneless, skinless chicken breasts, cut into ¾-inch pieces

1 tablespoon olive oil

1 tablespoon unsalted butter

FOR THE CILANTRO CREAM

1 cup heavy cream

½ cup packed cilantro

1 teaspoon kosher salt

FOR THE TOPPINGS

4 ounces feta cheese, crumbled

1½ cups (6 ounces) fresh mozzarella cheese, torn into bite-sized pieces

2 tablespoons plus 2 teaspoons canola oil

4 large eggs

¼ cup chopped cilantro

TO MAKE THE BREAD: In the bowl of an electric stand mixer, whisk the flour, salt, sugar, and oil. Fit the mixer with the dough hook attachment and position the bowl on the stand. Mix on low speed. Add the beer and mix on medium speed for 5 minutes or until the dough pulls away from the sides of the bowl and forms a smooth, elastic ball, scraping down the sides and bottom of the bowl as needed. Cover the bowl and set the dough aside for 20 minutes.

TO MAKE THE CHICKEN: In a medium bowl, mix together the ginger, garlic, salt, curry powder, garam masala, and turmeric. Add the chicken pieces and toss to coat.

Heat a large, heavy-bottomed sauté pan over high heat. Once the pan is hot, add the oil and butter. When the butter has melted, add the chicken and cook for 3 minutes or just until golden brown, turning as needed. Set the chicken aside to cool completely.

TO MAKE THE CILANTRO CREAM: In a blender, combine the cream, cilantro, and salt and pulse until smooth and pale green. Do not overblend, or the cream will curdle. Set aside.

TO MAKE THE FLATBREADS WITH TOPPINGS: Place 2 baking stones on the bottom rack of the oven and preheat the oven to 500°F.

Divide the dough into 4 pieces. Working with 1 piece at a time, roll out the dough into thin 12 x 6-inch ovals. Spread ¼ cup of the cilantro cream over each flatbread. Top each with the feta, mozzarella, and chicken. Transfer the flatbreads to the baking stones and bake for 8 minutes or until the breads are brown on the bottom and the cheese is melted.

Meanwhile, set a small, heavy-bottomed nonstick sauté pan over medium heat until hot. Add 2 teaspoons of the canola oil and crack 1 egg into the pan. Cover and cook for 3 minutes, or until the egg white is set and golden brown on the bottom and the yolk thickens but is still fluid. Transfer the fried egg to a plate and repeat with the remaining oil and eggs to fry 4 eggs total.

Sprinkle the cilantro over the flatbreads, then set the fried eggs on top and serve immediately.

THE VIRTUES OF STONE

A pizza stone will give your flatbread the closest possible taste to a true brick oven–baked bread. The stone retains more heat than, say, a pizza pan, resulting in a crispier crust. After each use, rinse with water only—avoid soap, as it will permeate the porous stone and impart a yucky dishwashing liquid flavor to all future breads.

NAAN SENSE

If you find yourself pressed for time, forgo making the crust from scratch and instead use ready-made *naan*, an Indian bread baked in a clay oven. This will lend an even more South Asian authenticity to your flatbread. You can find naan in specialty markets or the international section of most grocery stores. Don't forget to buy an extra pack to eat with Chicken Tikka Masala (page 105).

SWEETBREAD NUGGETS WITH BOK CHOY

⟡ **Like many American kids,** I grew up eating chicken nuggets. Whether for school lunch, from McDonald's, or from a bag in the freezer, chicken nuggets doused in ketchup were a childhood comfort. Now that I'm much older and just a tad more responsible, I prefer learning to make everything myself; cooking for yourself is the only way to control exactly what goes into your food, and this tends to result in healthier choices.

I had my first taste of sweetbreads at a little gastropub in Austin, after I returned for a post-college visit. The server said they were a house favorite, and so I ordered them, not knowing exactly what they were. I was expecting a plate of sugary pastries, but what I got instead reminded me of chicken nuggets. They were bite-sized chunks of sweetbreads—whatever those things were—breaded and fried and quite delicious. But then again, when is something breaded and fried *not* delicious? It wasn't until I looked up *sweetbreads* in the dictionary that I learned they were an animal's thymus gland. Being Asian and having grown up immersed in the nose-to-tail philosophy long before it was trendy in America, I wasn't at all offended by what I'd eaten. Instead I was excited to discover another edible part of an animal.

My curiosity paid off when I encountered the offal Mystery Box Challenge on *MasterChef* Season 3. Beef tongue? Bull's testicles? Lamb's brains? Forget 'em. Thinking of those nuggets from the gastropub, I went straight for the sweetbreads. Unsure as to what to do with them, I did what I always do: When in doubt, I bust out the bread crumbs and the deep fryer. It's a cooking method that makes even guts taste good. So don't let those thymus glands intimidate you. Bread. Fry. Eat. Finger-lickin' good.

SERVES 4

FOR THE SWEETBREADS

2 cups whole milk

1 small onion, sliced

3 cloves garlic, minced

1 small shallot, finely diced

4 fresh bay leaves

½ teaspoon Chinese five-spice powder

12 ounces sweetbreads, membranes removed, cut into 2-inch pieces

1 cup all-purpose flour

½ teaspoon garlic powder

½ teaspoon kosher salt plus additional for the eggs

½ teaspoon freshly ground black pepper plus additional for the eggs

6 large eggs

2½ cups panko (Japanese) bread crumbs

½ teaspoon red-pepper flakes

Canola oil

FOR THE BOK CHOY

> 4 slices bacon, diced
>
> 4 small bok choy, separated and cleaned
>
> Soy-Chile Dipping Sauce (page 174)

FOR THE GARNISH (OPTIONAL)

> 1 jalapeño chile pepper, thinly sliced into rounds (wear plastic gloves when handling)
>
> 1 scallion, thinly sliced
>
> 4 sprigs cilantro

TO MAKE THE SWEETBREADS: In a large bowl, stir the milk, onion, garlic, shallot, bay leaves, and 1/4 teaspoon of the five-spice powder. Add the sweetbreads and marinate for 20 minutes.

In a separate large bowl, whisk the flour, garlic powder, 1/2 teaspoon salt, 1/2 teaspoon pepper, and the remaining 1/4 teaspoon five-spice powder to blend. In a wide shallow bowl, whisk the eggs to blend, then season to taste with salt and pepper and set aside. In another wide shallow bowl, mix the panko and red-pepper flakes and set aside.

Remove the sweetbreads from the marinade and pat dry. Roll the sweetbreads in the flour mixture to coat, then submerge them in the egg mixture to coat. Lift the sweetbreads from the egg mixture, allowing the excess egg to drip back into the bowl. Coat the sweetbreads in the panko mixture. Set the sweetbreads aside for 5 minutes.

In a large wok or pot over medium-high heat, heat 3 inches of oil to 375°F. Toss the sweetbreads in the panko to coat again. Working in batches, fry the sweetbreads for 3 minutes or until they are browned on all sides. Using a slotted spoon, remove the sweetbreads from the wok and drain on paper towels.

TO MAKE THE BOK CHOY: Meanwhile, heat a large sauté pan over medium-high heat. Add the bacon and cook, stirring frequently, for 3 minutes or until some of the fat is rendered. Using a slotted spoon, remove the bacon pieces from the pan and discard. Add the bok choy to the pan and cook, stirring frequently, for 2 minutes or until crisp-tender.

Lay the bok choy on 4 long rectangular plates. Place the sweetbreads on top of the bok choy, across the whole length of the plate. Fill 4 small ramekins or bowls with the Soy-Chile Dipping Sauce and place them at one end of the plates.

TO GARNISH: Garnish with the jalapeño chile pepper slices, scallion, and cilantro, if desired.

HANDLING OFFAL

Most offal requires long soaks and tedious preparation in order to prepare it for eating. Of course, I did not have that luxury when it came to the timed challenge on *MasterChef*. I found that as long as I meticulously removed all of the sweetbreads' membranes and soaked them in a milk bath for at least 20 minutes prior to cooking, that did the trick.

CARAMELIZED CHICKEN WINGS

✧ **Because I'm from the South** and attended the University of Texas at Austin, it's only natural that American football has been part of my life. From games between college rivals to the NFL season, culminating in the Super Bowl, there are many occasions between September and February to come together, cheer—and eat. Wherever a bunch of passionate fans gather in one place—whether they're shouting at the referee over unfair calls or pumping their fists at touchdowns—there are hungry people.

Wings are to watching football on TV as popcorn is to watching movies in the theater. But sometimes, the typical buffalo wing can get a little boring. Here's a recipe that takes the chicken wing and dresses it up with such Vietnamese staples as fish sauce, garlic, and cilantro. (Little-known fact: Because they are one of my favorite flavor profiles, having cooked with them frequently on the show, I got images of these three ingredients tattooed on me to commemorate my experience at *MasterChef*.) Your love for fish sauce, garlic, and cilantro may not run as deep as mine, but I guarantee you'll score some points with these wings.

SERVES 6

½ cup fish sauce

½ cup sugar

2 tablespoons ketchup

6 cloves garlic

Zest of 1 lime

3 pounds chicken wings, cut at joints, with tips trimmed and discarded

2 tablespoons canola oil plus additional for frying

1 cup cornstarch

2 red chile peppers, seeded and finely chopped (wear plastic gloves when handling)

1½ tablespoons finely chopped cilantro

½ tablespoon finely chopped mint

In a large bowl, combine the fish sauce, sugar, ketchup, 4 crushed cloves garlic, and lime zest. Divide the chicken wings into 2 large resealable plastic bags. Pour half the marinade into each, seal, and shake well to coat. Refrigerate for at least 3 hours, turning once.

In a small skillet, heat the 2 tablespoons oil over medium-high heat. Add 2 cloves minced garlic and cook for 2 minutes or until soft and fragrant. Transfer the garlic to a paper towel–lined plate to drain.

Fill a deep pot with 3 inches of oil and heat to 350°F. Set 2 wire racks over paper bags. Place the cornstarch in a shallow rimmed bowl. Shake excess marinade off the chicken and set the marinade aside. Dredge the wings in the cornstarch and shake off the excess. Fry the wings for 10 minutes or until golden and cooked through. Transfer to the racks and let drain onto the paper bags.

Pour the reserved marinade into a medium saucepan, and bring it to a boil. Reduce the heat and cook until the mixture thickens to a syrupy consistency. Remove from the heat and stir in the chile peppers, cilantro, and mint. Toss with the chicken wings to coat.

BROWN-BAGGING IT

To drain the wings of excess oil after frying, place them on wire racks over paper bags or baking sheets. I set mine on racks typically used to cool cakes and cookies, letting the extra oil drip onto old grocery sacks. This way, the chicken won't sit in its own sad grease and get soggy. In order to keep the first batch of wings warm while you fry the rest, set the wire racks over baking sheets (rather than bags) in a 250°F oven.

CANDIED BACON

✧ **How do I love thee, bacon?** Let me count the ways. I am disappointed to say that the first strip of bacon I ever had was not until high school. But it's been a full-on pork lovefest ever since.

Yes, bacon adds a rich, salty component to any dish, but my first experience with bacon involved eating it on its own as a snack, and that's still my favorite way. And when it's coated with pecans and sugar, all the better. The result is a crunchy, salty, sweet concoction. You can substitute turkey bacon for the pork bacon, if desired.

SERVES 4

18 whole pecans

12 slices bacon

$\frac{1}{3}$ cup light brown sugar

Freshly ground black pepper

Place a rack in the middle of the oven and preheat the oven to 400°F. Line a baking sheet with parchment paper or aluminum foil. Place the pecans in the bowl of a food processor and pulse until coarsely crushed into $\frac{1}{8}$-inch pieces.

In a medium bowl, combine the bacon and pecans and toss. Add the brown sugar and pepper and toss to coat. Arrange the bacon slices in a single layer on the baking sheet. Sprinkle any leftover pecans and sugar from the bowl over the bacon. Top with another layer of parchment or foil and cover squarely with a second baking sheet to flatten the bacon as it cooks.

Bake until the bacon is crisp, 14 to 16 minutes. Halfway through cooking, turn the bacon, using tongs, dragging it through the syrup in the bottom of the pan. Bake for another 5 minutes if the strips have not darkened. Serve by the strip or break up into 2-inch pieces and serve in a bowl.

BACON LOVE

Candied Bacon can be eaten by itself as a snack or added to other dishes to amp up the flavor. For example, cut the slices up into 1-inch pieces and toss with Roasted Brussels Sprouts with Caramelized Fish Sauce (page 136). Add a slice or two to Mushroom and Onion Burgers (page 98). Or you can finely chop the bacon and use it to top a scoop of Browned Butter Ice Cream (page 161) or go classic and eat it with a breakfast of Sunny-Side-Up Eggs with Toast (page 56).

SYMPHONIC SASHIMI

✧ **This gorgeous dish** is inspired by one I had at Graham Elliot's restaurant in Chicago. The first time I had raw fish, in college, I hated it. But I believe in second chances, and the next time I tried sushi, I loved it. When accompanied by the traditional shredded radish, soy sauce, and wasabi, sashimi is like a sultry, mellow jazz tune. When served with passion fruit, cocoa nibs, and avocado mousse, sashimi becomes a symphony. On *MasterChef* Season 3, we were given this dish to replicate during an Elimination Challenge. Not being able to see it, I had to feel and taste all the components to try to figure out how to re-create Chef's white tuna sashimi. This recipe is what I came up with, and while it may not be an exact match, it still came out pretty damn good.

SERVES 4

FOR THE AVOCADO MOUSSE

1 firm but ripe avocado, peeled and pitted

1½ tablespoons fresh lemon juice

1 tablespoon sour cream

½ teaspoon wasabi powder

1 teaspoon kosher salt plus additional to taste

FOR THE PLANTAIN CHIPS

Canola oil

1 small green plantain

Kosher salt

FOR THE TUNA

16 slices (2 x 1½ x ¼-inch) white tuna

2 radishes, sliced into paper-thin rounds

1 scallion (dark green part only), very thinly sliced on a sharp bias

2 passion fruits

1 tablespoon cocoa nibs

2 teaspoons Maldon sea salt

2 teaspoons extra-virgin olive oil

TO MAKE THE AVOCADO MOUSSE: In a small food processor, combine the avocado, lemon juice, sour cream, wasabi, and 1 teaspoon kosher salt and blend until smooth. Season to taste with more salt. Transfer the mousse to a pastry bag fitted with a small plain tip and refrigerate.

TO MAKE THE PLANTAIN CHIPS: In a medium, heavy-bottomed saucepan over medium heat, heat 1 to 2 inches of oil to 375°F. Peel the plantain, then cut it in half lengthwise. Cut 1 half on a sharp bias into 16 paper-thin slices. Using a round cookie cutter, cut each slice into half-moons. Cover and refrigerate the leftover plantain half for another use. Working in batches, fry the slices for 3 minutes or until golden brown. Using a slotted spoon, transfer the chips to paper towels to drain. Season with salt.

TO ASSEMBLE THE TUNA: Lay 4 tuna slices on each of 4 plates. Pipe a small mound of the avocado mousse alongside each slice. Lay 1 radish slice against each mound of mousse and garnish with the scallion. Cut the passion fruits in half and spoon their pulp, juice, and seeds over the tuna. Sprinkle with the cocoa nibs and sea salt. Drizzle the oil evenly over the tuna and serve immediately with the plantain chips.

A GOOD KNIFE: A CHEF'S BEST FRIEND

On my last trip to Japan, my friend booked us a reservation at *her* friend's sushi restaurant. When given a choice, always take the seat at the bar; you'll get more personalized service from the sushi chef, and it's always a mind-blowing experience to watch a really good chef put together your sushi. (In my case, I chat with the chef, since I can't watch.) As the chef sliced fish after fish, I couldn't help but wonder about the knife he was using. I had the guts to ask him how much it cost. He paused, obviously converting yen to dollars in his head, and then answered in broken, endearing English, "One thousand dollars." Realistically, we average home cooks neither can afford nor really need a thousand-dollar sushi knife. But what you absolutely can't compromise on is a very sharp one, and the longer the blade, the better. Cut against the grain of the fish, starting with the part of the knife closest to the handle and pulling the fish toward you as you slice in one long, continuous motion. Do not use the knife like a saw, or the result will be a badly beaten piece of sashimi. If you've reached the tip of your knife and the piece is still attached to the whole fillet, carefully pick up the knife and start the slice again at the part of the blade closest to you.

NOT JUST ANY OLD FISH

Make sure you're using sashimi- or sushi-grade fish whenever you're going to consume it raw. You can find it at gourmet markets and top-quality fish markets. Ask your fishmonger for sashimi- or sushi-grade fish only.

MY LAST MEAL
The First Course

People often ask me what my favorite dish is, and I always reply, "Dish? As in singular? How about dishes, plural?" It's hard for me to decide what I love to eat most. I do love variety, and what I choose to eat always depends on the mood I'm in.

"All right. What are your favorite dishes, then?"

I've thought about this question a lot, asking myself what would be on the table at my last meal. Naturally, it would comprise several courses, each a small plate containing just a few bites so as not to make me full before I finished the last course. The first one, I always say, would be sashimi.

On the first day of a recent trip to Tokyo, I woke up at 3:30 in the morning to trek across town to the Tsukiji fish market, where 1½ hours later, the fish auction would begin. The wholesale fish market in Japan is no joke—a bluefin tuna recently sold for over $700,000 (and that's in US dollars, not Japanese yen!). I waited in line for 3 hours to get a seat at a tiny sushi bar where there are no menus because the chef serves sushi pieces prepared from whatever fresh fish he scored wholesale that morning. It meant I didn't have a choice in what I ate, but what I love to do when dining in the presence of great chefs is freely place my gastronomical fate in their hands. My companions and I sat elbow-to-elbow with strangers, all of us chewing quietly, enraptured by the rare occasion of being able to eat the freshest yet cheapest sushi in the world. With the sun rising behind us through the window outside, it felt like a near-sacred experience. I can't recall a single thing in my life that got me out of bed at 3:30 in the morning to stand in line for 3 hours. But raw fish got me to do it. And I've never regretted it.

(For the Second Course, see page 42.)

SEAWEED RICE ROLLS
Kimbap

✧ *Kimbap,* literally translated, means "seaweed rice" and is the Korean version of a sushi roll. Because they're neatly packaged finger foods, kimbap are often toted along on picnics and road trips. I recall a few summers ago when I went to an amusement park with friends, and we sat down to a lunch of seaweed rice rolls that we had brought along. The surrounding families gazed from their own bologna and cheese sandwiches to our colorful seaweed rice rolls, and I could feel the envy emanating from their eyes. I love these as a quick snack or simple meal. But because they don't keep well, be sure to eat them all up. To make the vegetarian version, skip the Spam.

MAKES 10 ROLLS (80 PIECES)

6 ounces Spam or ham,
cut into ½-inch-thick slices

4 cups Korean or Japanese white rice

2½ tablespoons sesame oil

Salt

4 eggs

1 tablespoon soy sauce

Freshly ground black pepper

1 teaspoon extra-light olive oil

10 sheets seaweed

10 sticks yellow pickled radish or 2–3 ounces,
cut into thin strips

In a large skillet over medium-high heat, fry the Spam, working in batches if necessary, and turning until golden on both sides, about 5 minutes. Transfer to a paper towel lined platter and set aside.

In a large saucepan, cook the rice according to package instructions with ¼ cup more water than called for. Alternatively, steam the rice in a rice cooker with ¼ cup more water than called for. The stickier the rice, the more intact it will remain in the roll. Set the rice aside to cool to room temperature. Once cooled, stir in the sesame oil and salt with a wooden spoon. Set aside.

In a small bowl, whisk the eggs until light yellow. Whisk in the soy sauce and pepper. In a medium skillet over medium heat, heat the olive oil until hot but not smoking. Pour the eggs into the skillet and cook until they begin to set. Once the edges are browned, flip the eggs over and cook until there is no liquid and the eggs are firm. Transfer to a cutting board, cool, and slice into ¼-inch-wide slices. Set aside.

Place a rolling mat on a clean work surface with the long edge facing you. Place a sheet of seaweed, shiny side down, on the rolling mat. Dip your fingers into some water, then pick up ½ cup of the rice and spread it from short edge to short edge, leaving about a 1-inch border at the top. Arrange the Spam strips along the length of the rice, 2 to 3 inches from the long side closest to you. Place strips of pickled radish on top of the Spam, followed by strips of egg. Beginning with the long edge facing you, roll the mat up over the filling, packing it tightly. Continue rolling until you reach the top. Using a very sharp knife, gently cut the roll into 8 equal pieces, taking care not to smash the roll. Continue until you have made and sliced 10 rolls.

Arrange the pieces, rice side up, on a platter and serve.

WHAT IF I DON'T LIKE SPAM?

You can use almost anything in your kimbap: imitation crab, real crab, Korean grilled beef (bulgogi), etc. Or go vegetarian with sautéed carrots, spinach, zucchini, or Korean spicy fermented cabbage (kimchi). Whatever you use, be sure to wring all the liquid from it—you want the ingredients to be as dry as possible to prevent the rolls from getting soggy and falling apart. The yellow pickled radish (danmuji), in my opinion, however, is a must for your kimbap; it can be found in many specialty Asian markets. I buy mine precut to the perfect size for kimbap, which helps minimize prep time.

CRAB COCKTAIL

✧ **During my early high school years,** summer vacations with my family had us road-tripping across the Mexican border, down the Baja to San Felipe, a quaint coastal town on the Sea of Cortez. We'd pitch our tents right on the beach and spend our days and nights on the bright white sand. The only time we'd leave the beach was when we got tired of our cold-cut sandwiches and ventured into town in search of something more enticing than ham and cheese. On one of these outings, I tasted my first seafood cocktail from a street vendor, who proudly served it up in a tin tumbler. My cousins and I sat on rickety stools and passed the cup around, so taken by the flavors that we ignored the splinters in our rear ends! The cocktail, loaded with the catches of the day, fresh veggies, and herbs, was cool and complex. It was love at first bite. Over my successive trips to Mexico, I have found that the best crab cocktails come from the street stalls; to my mind, all seafood tastes better eaten outdoors.

Dungeness crabs are one of the meatiest of all varieties of crab, but even so, expect only about 25 percent of the crab's bulk weight to be meat. For this recipe, a crab of roughly 1½ pounds is needed to produce the 6 ounces of meat required.

SERVES 4

FOR THE CRAB

1 stalk celery, sliced

½ red onion, diced

2 cloves garlic, sliced

1½ teaspoons kosher salt

1 live (1½–1¾-pound) Dungeness crab

FOR THE SAUCE

1 cup tomato-vegetable juice (such as V8), chilled

¼ cup finely diced red onion

¼ cup finely diced celery plus 4 small stalks celery for garnish

¼ cup finely diced tomato

2 tablespoons finely diced scallions

1 tablespoon finely diced Fresno chile pepper (wear plastic gloves when handling)

1 tablespoon finely diced jalapeño chile pepper (wear plastic gloves when handling)

1 tablespoon minced cilantro

Juice of 2 limes

4 dashes hot sauce

Kosher salt and freshly ground black pepper

1 avocado, peeled, pitted, and finely diced

TO MAKE THE CRAB: In a large heavy stockpot, combine the celery, onion, garlic, and salt. Fill the pot with water. Bring the water to a boil over high heat. Using tongs, add the crab, then cover the pot and cook for 2 minutes or until the crab's shell is bright red. Transfer the crab to a large bowl of ice water and set aside until cold. Remove all the crabmeat from the shell (you should have about 6 ounces of crabmeat). Cover and refrigerate until ready to serve.

TO MAKE THE SAUCE: In a large bowl, combine the tomato-vegetable juice, onion, diced celery, tomato, scallions, Fresno chile pepper, jalapeño chile pepper, cilantro, lime juice, and hot sauce. Season to taste with salt and black pepper. Fold in half of the avocado and the reserved crabmeat.

Divide the mixture among 4 small serving bowls. Garnish with the remaining avocado and the small stalks of celery and serve immediately.

CONQUERING THE CRAB

When dealing with a live crab, use tongs to grab the crustacean from behind; this keeps the pincher claws at arm's length. Blanch by thrusting the crab briefly into boiling water until the shell turns red and immediately transferring it to an ice bath to stop the cooking process. The ice bath is vital, as overcooked shellfish is rubbery and no fun to eat.

WHEN LIFE HANDS YOU LIVE CRAB, YOU MAKE CRAB COCKTAIL

That's exactly what I did with the live Dungeness crab on *MasterChef* Season 3. Whenever you are working with food so fresh it's still kicking, you want to retain its essential flavor by barely cooking it, using a very simple preparation method that involves few steps and few ingredients. This philosophy can be applied to any high-quality product, whether it be seafood, meat (think how a juicy aged rib eye is best when seared and seasoned only with salt, pepper, and a pat of butter), or fruits and vegetables (imagine eating seasonal produce lightly grilled or, better, right off the vine). If live Dungeness crab is a bit out of your price range, try substituting blue crab or shrimp—just about any shellfish will do.

SALMON POKE

✧ **Some things in life are better left alone:** a sleeping bear, beehives, fruitcake, and a fresh fillet of salmon. I loathe cooked salmon, but raw? That's an entirely different story. During an Elimination Challenge on *MasterChef* Season 3, Felix, who had the advantage, gave me the big, beautiful salmon because, he exclaimed, "I love Christine!" The judges agreed that the salmon was a great fish to be assigned because it was so prized. It was huge, delicious, and versatile.

As soon as I realized I'd gotten the salmon, though, my heart sank. My gut was telling me to slice off the belly and serve it sashimi-style (see "My Last Meal: The First Course," page 23), but I remembered the judges' disdain for some of the raw foods previously served to them. I sliced off a bright pink marbleized chunk of the salmon belly in case I decided to go with my instincts. But the grim, shaking heads of Gordon, Graham, and Joe clouded my judgment, and out of fear, I botched my beautiful salmon by cooking it too long in the oven. Sure enough, all three judges claimed it was the worst dish I'd cooked so far in the competition.

Right then and there, I vowed never again to worry about what they wanted and instead always to follow my intuition. Even if it was something simple, so long as it was yummy, that's all that mattered. Sashimi is not the only method of eating raw fish. *Poke* (correctly pronounced "poh-keh") is a Hawaiian favorite. I created this as a tribute to Felix and her Hawaiian heritage, a way of saying thank you for giving me the salmon out of love. And to Gordon, Graham, and Joe, here it is: my salmon redemption.

Make sure you're using sashimi- or sushi-grade fish here. It is generally available at gourmet markets and Asian specialty stores. Consult with the fishmonger if you're unsure. If you prefer to stick to the traditional Hawaiian recipe, use ahi tuna steak instead of salmon. While it's meant to be eaten as a light salad just by itself, I like to serve my poke on something starchy, such as rice crackers, shrimp chips, sesame crackers, or—my favorite—wonton crisps. To make the poke even more filling, spoon some on top of a bit of rice and wrap it in a 3 x 5-inch sheet of nori.

SERVES 8 TO 10 AS AN APPETIZER

2 pounds fresh sashimi-grade salmon, cut into ¼-inch cubes

1 cup light soy sauce

2 tablespoons sesame oil

¾ cup thinly sliced scallions

1 tablespoon toasted sesame seeds

1 tablespoon seaweed seasoning (optional)

2 teaspoons crushed red pepper or to taste

In a medium bowl, combine the salmon, soy sauce, sesame oil, scallions, sesame seeds, seaweed seasoning (if using), and crushed red pepper. Stir to combine thoroughly. Cover and refrigerate for at least 2 hours. Serve chilled.

HELP—I CAN'T FIND SEAWEED SEASONING IN THE SPICE AISLE!

Seaweed, or nori, seasoning generally consists of sesame seeds and finely chopped dried seaweed, among other spices. You may find it in the international aisle of the grocery store, in the Japanese section, near the panko bread crumbs. It is also available in Asian specialty markets in the condiment aisle.

Chapter 2

A Bowl of Comfort

As a child, I ate the majority of my meals out of bowls the way most Vietnamese families do. My mama ladled noodle soups and curries into bowls bigger than my face, while steamed rice, fried rice, rice soups, and just about anything eaten over rice was served up in smaller vessels that adults could hold in one hand. As a small girl, I struggled to go one-handed but always gave in, cupping both my hands around the bowl as I brought it up to my lips for slurping. In Western homes, I would have been reprimanded for eating this way and making such noises, but it's customary at the

Vietnamese table to sip your soup loudly (it indicates your satisfaction) and to lift a bowl from table to mouth.

Most of the recipes that follow take me straight back to those days when there was always a pot of steaming broth on the stove in our home kitchen. While my mama invariably prepared Vietnamese soups and rices, I came to love some of the classic American soups and stews, too, clam chowder being one of my favorites. But it's the Westernized Eastern dish of ketchup fried rice, which fuses the two culinary cultures in which I was raised, that I turn to again and again; it's addictive and, yes, endlessly comforting.

I've found that serving up any dish in a bowl instantly conjures a convivial atmosphere. I have a loose set of rules when it comes to the method in which I present my soups, stews, curries, and rices. I always serve my mama's tomato soup as well as sour prawn soup out of a tureen set in the center of the table. Each person ladles some soup from the large vessel into a smaller personal bowl filled with rice. When noodle soups, curries, porridges, and chowders are on the menu, I serve them in medium- to large-sized individual bowls, while those dishes without broth—fried rice and stir-fried noodles—call for family-style platters from which each diner spoons a portion into a smaller bowl. However you decide to serve and eat them, the dishes in this chapter will bring warmth, comfort, and, I hope, the impulse to slurp.

MY MAMA'S HUMBLE TOMATO SOUP
Canh Cà Chua của Mẹ

✧ **This is ultimate peasant comfort food:** a simple aromatic broth that is more delicate than traditional tomato soups yet wonderfully soothing. My mama always served this when she wanted to complement a heartier main course such as Clay Pot Catfish (page 72) or Braised Pork Riblets (page 66). In the winter, we ate it piping hot, but in the summer, a chilled version cooled us off. Either way, it's light, healthy, and easy to whip up. My favorite way to eat it? Ladled over a bowl of steamed jasmine rice.

SERVES 6

1 tablespoon extra-light olive oil

2 cloves garlic, minced

6 ripe garden tomatoes, blanched, peeled, and cut into wedges

1 quart Poultry Stock (page 172) or low-sodium chicken broth

2 cups water

2 tablespoons fish sauce

1 bird's-eye chile pepper, seeded and chopped (optional; wear plastic gloves when handling)

Kosher salt and freshly ground black pepper

Chopped scallions

Chopped cilantro

In a medium saucepan over medium-high heat, heat the olive oil. Add the garlic and cook, stirring frequently, until fragrant, 2 minutes. Add the tomato wedges and cook, stirring constantly, for 2 minutes or until they begin to break apart. Add the stock, water, fish sauce, chile pepper (if using), and salt and pepper and bring to a boil. Reduce the heat to low and simmer, covered, for 30 to 45 minutes. Taste the soup and adjust the fish sauce, salt, and black pepper. Ladle into bowls and garnish with the scallions and cilantro. Serve hot or chilled.

SCORE, BLANCH, PEEL

To remove the skins from the tomatoes without butchering them, try this:

1. Bring a large pot of water to a boil.

2. Using a knife, score the bottom of each tomato with a small X.

3. Prepare an ice-water bath.

4. Blanch the tomatoes by placing them in the boiling water for 25 seconds.

5. Plunge the tomatoes into the ice-water bath to stop the cooking.

6. Once cooled, peel the tomato skins, starting from the scored Xs.

RICE PORRIDGE WITH CHICKEN
Cháo Gà

✧ **This warming stew is the Asian version** of the classic American chicken soup with rice. Every time I had a cold or the flu as a child, my mama would whip up a pot of this for me. When winter rolls around I crave it, particularly when I feel a cold coming on. It's hearty and sustaining yet easy on the stomach, and it's quick and easy to make. The longer you simmer the rice, the softer it gets; I like my rice quite bloated and mushy, which is why I give a range for the cooking time. Taste it at the 15-minute mark and decide for yourself from there.

SERVES 4

1 cup jasmine rice

6 cups Poultry Stock (page 172) or low-sodium chicken broth

1 boiled chicken breast, shredded

½ medium onion, finely chopped

1 piece (1 inch) fresh ginger, peeled and minced

2 tablespoons fish sauce or to taste

Freshly ground black pepper

4 scallions, thinly sliced

3 sprigs cilantro, finely chopped (optional)

In a medium saucepan, combine the rice, stock, chicken, onion, and ginger and bring to a low boil. Reduce the heat and add the fish sauce. Cover and simmer for 15 to 20 minutes, or until the rice is the desired consistency. Season to taste with black pepper and additional fish sauce. Garnish with the scallions and cilantro, if desired, and serve hot.

ONE-POT WONDER

I always make this soup after I've made a flavorful stock from the Thanksgiving turkey bones. Think of it as the Vietnamese version of pot pie in that you can throw almost anything you find in your fridge into this porridge. This recipe is basic; add whatever meat you please, use soy sauce instead of fish sauce, try garlic instead of ginger, or swap out the poultry stock and meat and use vegetable stock along with chopped vegetables for a vegetarian version.

TO YOUR HEALTH

I'm never sure if you feed a cold and starve a fever or the other way around, but I do know that a bowl of cháo gà can heal whatever is ailing you. Call it the Vietnamese penicillin, but it has everything a healing soup should have: a soothing texture and health-promoting ingredients such as ginger, which can alleviate nausea and stomach upset. Skip the sodium-laced can of chicken noodle soup and, instead, nourish yourself back to health with a bowl of Mama's medicine.

MY MAMA'S CHICKEN NOODLE SOUP
Phở Gà của Mẹ

✧ **There is nothing like a steaming hot bowl** of this noodle soup on a cold winter day. But phở is not just one of those things I love to eat when the frost is settling on the leaves outside; it is simply one of my favorite dishes *ever*. It doesn't matter if it's a scalding Houston summer afternoon—I'll still gladly sweat over my bowl of phở.

My mama made the best phở I'd ever had in my life. And I'm not just saying that because she was my mama. It was so good that her friends used to constantly urge her to open a noodle shop.

Years after she died, when I began trying to piece together her recipes, I asked my dad about her phở. He told me she'd jotted down a list of ingredients somewhere, but the notes were forever lost.

While my mama usually made the better-known beef version, it was her phở gà—chicken noodle soup—that I loved more. The stock is lighter in flavor but still packed with umami. It took me years before I finally mustered up the courage to try to replicate her recipe. I sometimes still imagine my mama standing over my shoulder and shaking her head in disapproval. I can only hope that my version of phở gà, inspired by hers, is half as good as the soup of my childhood.

You'll notice that I char the whole onions and piece of ginger and dry-roast the spices here. In doing so, I am coaxing every bit of sweetness and flavor from the ingredients, which translates to a more flavorful stock. If, like me, you are an ardent fan of dark meat, use 6 chicken leg quarters in lieu of a whole chicken.

SERVES 8

FOR THE STOCK

2 medium yellow onions

1 piece (4 inches) ginger

1 star anise

2 tablespoons coriander seeds

4 whole cloves

1 medium whole chicken, trimmed

3 pounds chicken necks, trimmed

5 quarts water

1 tablespoon salt

2 tablespoons sugar

¼ cup fish sauce

FOR THE PHỞ

3 ounces medium-width flat rice noodles

1 small red onion, sliced into paper-thin half-moons and soaked in cold water

3 scallions, green parts only, thinly sliced

¼ cup finely chopped cilantro

1 bunch whole cilantro

Freshly ground black pepper

Bean sprouts

Thai basil

Mint

Cilantro

Jalapeño chile pepper slices
(wear plastic gloves when handling)

Lime wedges

Hoisin sauce

Sriracha sauce

TO MAKE THE STOCK: On a grill or gas stove, place the whole onions and ginger directly on the grates over a medium open flame. Cook, using tongs to turn occasionally, until all sides are charred, 15 minutes. Remove from the heat and let cool slightly.

Meanwhile, in a small skillet set over medium heat, roast the star anise, coriander seeds, and whole cloves for 2 minutes or until fragrant, shaking the pan occasionally.

Rinse the onions under warm water to remove the charred skin. Peel the ginger, halve it, and gently smash it, using the side of a knife.

Remove the wings from the chicken and add them to the chicken necks. Remove the gizzards and reserve them for another use (see Dirty Rice, page 146). Using a meat cleaver, chop the chicken necks to expose the marrow.

In a large stockpot, combine the whole chicken, the necks and wings, and enough water to cover. Bring to a boil and continue boiling for 3 minutes or until the chicken is parboiled. Transfer the chicken, necks, and wings to a colander and rinse thoroughly to remove scum. Rinse out the stockpot.

Place the whole chicken, necks, wings, and charred onions and ginger back into the stockpot. Add the water to the pot and heat until the liquid is just about to boil. Do not bring to a full boil or the stock will be cloudy. Reduce the heat and simmer, skimming the surface with a spoon.

Place the star anise, coriander seeds, and cloves in a sachet or a mesh spice ball and add it to the pot, along with the salt, sugar, and fish sauce. If necessary, add water to just cover the ingredients. Simmer, uncovered, for 25 minutes.

Remove the whole chicken from the stockpot and set it aside to cool. Cut the 2 breasts from the bone, as well as the 2 leg quarters with the thighs and drumsticks attached. Cover them in plastic wrap and refrigerate.

Return the chicken carcass to the stockpot. Taste the stock and adjust the salt, sugar, and fish sauce. Simmer for 2 hours more, using a spoon to skim the surface occasionally. Do not allow it to boil, or the stock will be murky. Remove from the heat, strain, and cool to room temperature. Cover and refrigerate overnight.

TO MAKE THE PHỞ: Remove any fat that has solidified on the surface of the stock, then return the pot to medium-low heat and bring the stock to a simmer. Taste it and adjust the salt, sugar, and fish sauce. Meanwhile, bring another large stockpot of water to a boil. Turn off the heat, add the rice noodles, and cover. Let sit for 10 minutes, or until the noodles are al dente. Drain and rinse under cold water.

Remove the chicken from the refrigerator and tear it into 2-inch pieces.

On a platter, arrange the bean sprouts, Thai basil, mint, cilantro, jalapeño chile pepper slices, and lime wedges. Divide the noodles among 8 soup bowls, followed by the chicken, red onion, scallions, and chopped and whole cilantro.

TO SERVE WITH THE GARNISHES AND CONDIMENTS: Ladle 2 cups of stock into each bowl. Season with freshly ground black pepper to taste and serve hot. Invite guests to help themselves to the garnishes and to the hoisin and Sriracha sauces.

A FEW NOTES ON PHỞ

Phở is so often mispronounced that I think it's worth including a brief tutorial here. If you say it as if it rhymes in this sentence—"I fo' sho' want some phở"—read on. *Phở* is pronounced "fuh," as in "fun," with an inquiring inflection at the end. Practice this, and you'll impress all the Vietnamese servers at the phở restaurants when you order in perfect Vietnamese

USING THE NOODLE

I grew up on dried noodle packages, but some cooks swear by the fresh ones. Prepare them the same way you would the dry packaged noodles, except reduce the amount of time they steep in hot water to just 1 minute. You'll see the majority of phở bowls using the small-width rice noodles, but my mama always made phở with a slightly wider, medium-width noodle. She was born in northern Vietnam, where phở originated, and it's traditional to use a slightly wider noodle in the soup. So as a tribute to my mama, I, too, always serve my phở with medium-width rice noodles. Look for an *M* on the package, which indicates a medium noodle, or, if you prefer, an *S* for small. There is not much difference; it's really a matter of preference. Never, however, use noodles marked *L* for phở; large-width rice noodles are generally used for stir-fried dishes such as Soy Sauce Stir-Fried Noodles (page 50).

CHICKEN CURRY
Cà Ri Gà

✧ **Every Asian country has its own curry.** The Vietnamese version, like many Southeast Asian dishes, boasts a spectrum of flavors: sour lemongrass, sweet coconut milk, fiery garlic and curry powder, and salty fish sauce. Cà ri gà is another childhood favorite of mine: I used to tear the accompanying bread into bite-sized pieces, drown them in my bowl, and then shovel spoonfuls of carrot, potato, chicken, and soggy bread into my mouth. In fact, I still eat cà ri gà exactly this way.

This stewlike curry is perfect for chasing the chill from your bones. I always eat it with slices of French bread—one of the many colonial marks France left on Vietnam—but you can also spoon it over rice noodles, egg noodles, or plain jasmine rice.

SERVES 6

2 tablespoons curry powder

1 teaspoon onion powder

1 teaspoon garlic powder

1 teaspoon salt

1 teaspoon freshly ground black pepper

2–3 pounds bone-in chicken legs and thighs, cut into bite-sized pieces

2 tablespoons canola oil

2 cloves garlic, minced

1 medium yellow onion, chopped

2 stalks lemongrass, cut into 3-inch pieces and smashed

3 medium Yukon Gold potatoes, peeled, each cut into 6 wedges

3 medium carrots, cut into 1-inch pieces

2 stalks celery, chopped

¼ cup fish sauce or to taste

1 quart Poultry Stock (page 172) low-sodium chicken broth or enough to cover ingredients

1 can (13.5 ounces) coconut milk

2 teaspoons cornstarch

Cilantro

In a small bowl, combine 1 tablespoon of the curry powder and all of the onion powder, garlic powder, salt, and pepper. Divide between 2 large resealable plastic bags. Divide the chicken between them, seal, and shake to coat. Refrigerate for at least 30 minutes.

In a large stockpot over medium-high heat, heat the oil. Add the garlic and onion and cook until soft and fragrant, 3 minutes. Add the remaining 1 tablespoon curry powder and stir for 30 seconds. Add the chicken and stir until coated all over in the curry mixture, 3 minutes. Add the lemongrass, potatoes, carrots, celery, fish sauce, stock, and coconut milk. If the chicken is not entirely covered in liquid, add more stock. Raise the heat to high, bring to a boil, cover, and reduce the heat to medium-low. Simmer until the vegetables are tender and the chicken is cooked through, 20 to 30 minutes. Meanwhile, combine the cornstarch with 2 teaspoons of water and stir to dissolve. Stir in the cornstarch mixture and cook for 2 minutes more. Garnish with the cilantro and serve with a baguette.

MY LAST MEAL
The Second Course

After indulging in sushi, I would follow it with a humble russet potato—cut into matchsticks, fried twice, and generously salted. What can I say? I love french fries. (See page 144 for my Double-Fried Fries.) Nothing comforts me quite like potatoes in any form, but I'd choose the all-American version. As embarrassing as it is to admit, my love for fries stems from memories of my trips to, yes, McDonald's. Those golden arches symbolized all that was good in life back then: meals that came with collectible toys, an over-the-top playground, cookies, soft-serve ice cream cones—and hot, golden french fries. I used to eat them one at a time (without ketchup—the purist in me started young), savoring each bite, under the glare of my mama, who absolutely abhorred how long it took me to get through the tiny pouch.

(For the Third Course, see page 70.)

PEANUT BUTTER OXTAIL STEW
Kare-Kare

✧ **Like many other teenagers,** I wanted to hang out at my best friend's house when I was in high school. This meant I spent many nights at his dinner table, helping myself to his mother's home-cooked Filipino food. I gobbled up her egg rolls, stir-fried noodles, and pork chops. But whenever oxtail was on the menu, I quietly shuddered and shied away. Imagine my surprise when I discovered it is a key ingredient in *phở bo*, the Vietnamese beef noodle soup I grew up eating.

I regretted never having given that oxtail a chance, so on a recent trip to New York, when my cousin suggested dinner at a Filipino restaurant, I was determined to make up for lost time. The oxtail stew was so good, I gnawed away on the bones. Here's my version, which features the classic trio of peanut sauce, vegetables, and slow-cooked oxtail. You can serve it on its own or over rice.

SERVES 6

3 pounds oxtail, cut into 1½-inch slices and rinsed

1 medium yellow onion, chopped

1 quart beef broth

2 tablespoons extra-light olive oil

3 cloves garlic, minced

1 eggplant, cubed

½ pound fresh French-style green beans (haricots verts), trimmed and washed

2 tablespoons dry roasted peanuts

¼ cup smooth peanut butter

¼ cup annatto seeds, soaked in ½ cup water

Salt and freshly ground black pepper

Shrimp paste

In a large stockpot, combine the oxtail, onion, and beef broth. Add enough water to just cover the ingredients. Bring to a boil. Reduce the heat to low, cover, and simmer for 3 hours or until the meat is fork-tender. Let cool to room temperature, then refrigerate overnight.

The next day, skim the fat that has solidified on the surface and return the broth to a simmer. Meanwhile, in a large pan over medium-high heat, heat the oil. Add the garlic and cook for 3 minutes or until fragrant. Add the eggplant and green beans and cook, stirring frequently, for 5 minutes or until al dente. Stir in the eggplant and add the vegetables to the oxtail mixture.

In a food processor, pulse the peanuts 4 times or until finely chopped. Add the peanuts, peanut butter, and liquid from the annatto seeds to the oxtail and vegetables. Stir to combine and let simmer until slightly thickened, 7 to 10 minutes. Season to taste with salt and pepper. Serve with shrimp paste.

PIN THE TAIL TO THE OX?

Oxtail is actually the tail of a cow. It is bony and gelatinous and typically braised or cooked into soups or stews. It is almost exclusively slow-cooked in order to tenderize and break down the tough muscle fibers. Oxtail is commonly used in African, Asian, Caribbean, South American, and European cuisines. You can usually find oxtail already sliced and packaged at Asian grocery stores.

SOUR PRAWN SOUP
Canh Chua Tôm

◇ **This soup is almost always served** with Clay Pot Catfish (page 72), because customarily it's made with the head and tail of the fish used in that dish.

I prefer to flavor my version with prawns rather than catfish for a couple of reasons: (1) I find the "prawn juice" sweeter and more palatable than catfish, and (2) there's just something a little unsettling about finding a catfish head floating in your soup.

While we often had My Mama's Humble Tomato Soup (page 34) for weeknight dinners, I opt for this because it's a bit more complex and has more textures. Since there were no tamarind pods in the *MasterChef* pantry the day I took on the spotted prawns Mystery Box Challenge, I didn't make a classic canh chua tôm. Instead, I made up something on the fly with this comfort soup in mind.

SERVES 6

1 tablespoon extra-light olive oil

1 shallot, thinly sliced

2 cloves garlic, minced

2 tomatoes, peeled and cut into wedges

2 stalks lemongrass, cut into 3-inch pieces and bruised

1 pineapple, peeled and cubed

2 tablespoons tamarind pulp

4 quarts water

1 pound whole prawns, peeled and deveined, heads and shells reserved for stock

2 Kaffir lime leaves

3 red chile peppers, seeded and finely chopped (wear plastic gloves when handling)

1 tablespoon palm sugar

3 tablespoons fish sauce

4 okra, cut into 1-inch pieces

1 cup bean sprouts

Cilantro

In a stockpot over medium-high heat, heat the oil. Add the shallot and garlic and cook for 3 minutes or until fragrant. Add the tomatoes, lemongrass, pineapple, and tamarind pulp and cook for 1 minute, stirring. Add the water and the reserved prawn heads and shells to the pot and bring to a boil. Reduce the heat to medium-low. Add the Kaffir lime leaves, chile peppers, palm sugar, and fish sauce. Simmer for 20 minutes to allow the flavors to be extracted from the shells.

Pass the soup through a chinois twice to achieve a clearer broth. Return the broth to the pot, along with the tomatoes and pineapple chunks. Discard everything else. Add the okra and bean sprouts and cook for 5 minutes or until the vegetables are tender. Add the prawns and cook until they are pink and just cooked through, 1 to 2 minutes. Remove from the heat. Ladle into bowls, garnish with the cilantro, and serve.

PRAWNS OR SHRIMP?

Prawns are shellfish that look like large shrimp. They're sweeter and meatier than their smaller relatives. They're more expensive than shrimp, so if you're feeling extravagant, go for it. But this soup tastes just as good with shrimp or, for that matter, the catfish head and tail from the Clay Pot Catfish (page 72) if you're on a tight budget.

CLAM CHOWDER

✧ **I first had clam chowder** about a decade ago while sitting on a bench on the touristy Fisherman's Wharf in San Francisco. It came in a sourdough bread bowl and was so thick, the chowder stuck to the roof of my mouth. It was like chewing drywall!

Several years later, while grocery shopping, I picked up a bag of littleneck clams because they were on sale, even though I had no idea what I was going to do with them. It was winter, when a nice, thick chowder is so satisfying, so I decided to try my hand at my own version, which is surprisingly simple to make. Serve this with a thick slice of bread from a rustic loaf.

If you like your chowder on the lighter side, forgo the heavy cream and use half-and-half or even milk. If, however, you prefer a thicker chowder, you can slowly stir in a tablespoon or so of flour right after you add the cream. Be careful, though, not to go too heavy on the flour, or your chowder can turn to sludge. If live clams aren't in your budget, use a 13.5-ounce can of clams with their juices and 2 to 3 cups of clam juice.

SERVES 6

2 tablespoons butter

1 medium onion, chopped

6 pounds littleneck clams, shells scrubbed and rinsed

$\frac{1}{2}$ cup dry white wine

4 slices bacon, cut into $\frac{1}{2}$-inch pieces

3 Yukon Gold potatoes, unpeeled, cut into medium dice

1 stalk celery, chopped

1 carrot, chopped

2 cups Poultry Stock (page 172) or low-sodium chicken broth

2 cups heavy cream

Salt and freshly ground black pepper

2 teaspoons thyme leaves

1 teaspoon finely chopped chives

In a large sauté pan over medium-high heat, melt 1 tablespoon of the butter. Add $\frac{1}{3}$ cup of the chopped onion and cook, stirring frequently, for 3 minutes or until fragrant and soft. Set aside 12 to 16 of the clams and add the rest to the pan. Add the wine, cover, and steam for 4 to 6 minutes, until the clams open. Turn off the heat and, with a slotted spoon, remove the cooked clams, saving the clam juice and onion mixture in the pan. Remove the cooked clams from their shells, chop them, and set them aside.

In a large soup pot over medium-high heat, cook the bacon until crisp. Remove the bacon with tongs or a slotted spoon and set it aside, leaving the rendered bacon fat in the pot.

Add the remaining 1 tablespoon butter to the pot and let it melt. Add the potatoes, celery, and carrot, and the remaining onion. Cook until the vegetables are slightly tender, 6 to 8 minutes, stirring frequently.

Pour the reserved clam juice and onion mixture from the sauté pan into the soup pot. Add the stock and, if necessary, add water to just cover the vegetables. Bring to a boil, then reduce the heat to medium-low and simmer, covered, for 10 to 15 minutes or until the potatoes are tender enough to pierce with a fork but do not break.

Stir in the reserved chopped clams and bacon and the cream. Cook for 10 minutes more, stirring occasionally, until the chowder returns to a simmer and thickens. Season with salt and pepper. Add the remaining live clams and simmer for 5 minutes or until the clams open. Ladle into bowls and garnish with the thyme and chives.

GIVE THE CLAMS A BATH

Clams, like other mollusks, require a good scrubbing before cooking. Under cold running water, use a toothbrush or nail brush to scrub the outside of each shell. This also gives you an opportunity to determine whether there are any dead clams in your batch. You'll want to discard these, as they may contain bacteria that you certainly don't want to eat. If a clam is gaping open, lightly tap its shell; if it's alive, it should close up. The opposite goes for cooked clams: If one refuses to open after all the others have been steamed open, don't try to pry it open. Toss it.

KETCHUP FRIED RICE
Cơm Chiên Sốt Cà Chua

✧ **I grew up eating fried rice.** What Asian kid didn't? Fried rice is the ultimate one-bowl comfort food. Like Meat Loaf (page 94), Rice Porridge with Chicken (page 35), or Prosciutto and Arugula Pizza (page 8), fried rice is a dish into which you can throw just about anything you have in your fridge or pantry. I've made fried rice before with Spam, rotisserie chicken, hot dogs, ham, mushrooms, corn, peas, carrots, pineapple, kimchi (Korean fermented cabbage)—you name it.

Because cold, day-old rice is preferable for this dish—newly steamed rice is too wet and will turn to mush in the wok—it's an ideal recipe for getting rid of leftovers. So don't throw out those cardboard containers of hard, old rice from Chinese takeouts past. In fact, don't throw out those fast-food ketchup packets either!

This version of ketchup fried rice is vegetarian, but you can add just about any meat to the dish for extra protein. It goes especially well with Shaking Beef (page 117).

SERVES 4

2 tablespoons ketchup

1 tablespoon soy sauce or Maggi sauce

2 tablespoons peanut oil

1 small yellow onion, finely chopped

2½ cups cooked rice, chilled for at least 30 minutes but preferably overnight

2 eggs

1 scallion, finely chopped

Salt and freshly ground black pepper

In a small bowl, mix together the ketchup and soy sauce until well incorporated. Set aside.

In a wok over high heat, heat the peanut oil. Add the onion and cook, stirring frequently, for 10 seconds or until fragrant. Add the rice, using your fingers to break it up before adding it to the wok. Stir-fry until the rice is coated evenly with the oil. Add the reserved ketchup and soy sauce mixture to the wok and stir-fry to distribute the sauce evenly throughout the rice.

Make a hole in the center of the wok by pushing the rice to the edges. Break the eggs into the center hole and scramble them quickly with a whisk until just cooked through. Add the scallion to the wok and stir the eggs and rice together until evenly incorporated. Season to taste with salt and pepper. Serve warm.

WHY ISN'T MY FRIED RICE AS GOOD AS THE CHINESE RESTAURANT'S?

Ever wonder how your favorite Chinese takeout joint makes such good rice? While fried rice is a simple dish, making it involves quite a bit of technique. First, a wok or at least a large stir-fry pan is essential. You also need a very hot fire: An open flame is ideal, but a gas stove is preferable to an electric one. The wok must be brought to a very high temperature in order to properly fry each grain of rice, so oils with high smoking points, like peanut oil, are best. When stir-frying, it's important not to overcrowd the wok to ensure even cooking. Cook the rice in batches if needed.

SOY SAUCE STIR-FRIED NOODLES
Pad See Ew

✧ **My college years** were a time for growth and experimentation. It was the first time I ate sushi, the first time I learned to like Indian food, and the first time I ever had Thai food. There was a Thai noodle shop next to campus with prices that suited my college student budget, and it was there that I tried my first bowl of Thai noodles doused in hot sauce. I was just beginning to learn how to cook, and I knew enough to know they weren't very good. I remember thinking with each disappointing bite that one day, I'd make better Thai noodles.

More than a decade later, I make Thai noodle dishes in my own kitchen. While *pad thai* is the more well-known Thai noodle stir-fry, it's the sweet, eggy, thick rice noodles of *pad see ew* that I prefer. *Pad see ew* literally means "fried with soy sauce," and you'll find this simple recipe great for those weeknights when you used to call for takeout.

SERVES 4

1 package (16 ounces) large-width flat rice noodles

6 teaspoons extra-light olive oil

2 cloves garlic, minced

$\frac{1}{2}$ pound pork loin, thinly sliced

3 tablespoons light soy sauce

1 tablespoon dark soy sauce

1 tablespoon sugar

6 stalks Chinese broccoli, halved lengthwise and cut into 2-inch pieces

3 eggs

White pepper

In a large pot, cook the rice noodles until slightly chewier than al dente, then drain them. In a large bowl, combine the noodles and $1\frac{1}{2}$ teaspoons of the oil. Toss well to coat evenly. Chill in the refrigerator for at least 30 minutes.

Heat a wok over high heat and add the remaining $4\frac{1}{2}$ teaspoons oil. Add the garlic and cook, stirring frequently, until fragrant. Add the pork and stir-fry until the meat loses all of its pink color.

Add the chilled rice noodles, using your fingers to break them apart before adding them to the wok. Add the light and dark soy sauces and the sugar. Stir-fry until the noodles are uniformly coated. Add the broccoli and continue stir-frying until the broccoli is fork-tender.

Push the noodles to the edges to make a hole in the center of the wok. Break the eggs into the center and scramble them with a whisk, cooking until they are firm. Toss the eggs and rice noodles together until thoroughly combined. Season with the pepper and serve.

INGREDIENT SWAP

The great thing about stir-fried dishes like this one is that you can use just about any ingredients you have on hand. No time to run to the store and get pork loin? Substitute with beef, chicken, or shrimp. For a vegetarian option, use fried tofu cubes or simply prepare the dish just with eggs.

SOY SAUCE: LIGHT OR DARK?

Ever wonder what the difference is between light and dark soy sauce? Light soy sauce is thin and lighter in color. Because of its saltier nature, it is used primarily for seasoning and dipping. Dark soy sauce, on the other hand, contains additives that make it darker and slightly sweeter than its lighter counterpart. Dark soy sauce is usually used during the cooking process to add color to the food.

Chapter 3

From My Mama's Kitchen

My mama never used recipes, so when she passed away, I had only my memory and senses to re-create her delicious food. In the years following her death, I made many attempts to reproduce the dishes she seemed to pull together without thinking, and I botched most of them. But I refused to give in and ultimately found my way to some of my childhood favorites. Choosing the dishes to include in this chapter wasn't easy—to properly pay homage to my mama, I'd have to catalog every single thing she ever made. Looking back, I am in awe of her ability to feed our family on little money and even less time. When my parents immigrated to America after the fall of Saigon in 1975, she taught high school English and became a social worker to help provide for our family. Despite full-time work, she always cooked for us, and the recipes that follow are among the handful that remain vivid in my memory. Here are the dishes that I remember watching her make as I sat on the stool pulled up to our kitchen island. She would hand me 10 chopsticks, instructing me to practice my addition and subtraction as she stood at the stove. I was invariably distracted by the aromas and sizzles coming from the other side of the counter. It was like watching a maestro: She was constantly lifting the lid off each pot, stirring with a wooden spoon, and wiping her hands on her signature apron, a chocolate brown one with a cartoon moose on the bib.

Curiously, my mama rarely, if ever, allowed me to help her in the kitchen. She was overly protective—sharp knives and open cans were, to her mind, too dangerous. The only time she let me near her work space was when she made egg rolls. I would peel the skins apart and lay them out on the cutting board. Once I mastered that, she let me fill and wrap the egg rolls myself. Frying them, of course, was off limits. Despite her reluctance, I eventually taught myself to cook, not out of rebellion but just the opposite. The nostalgia for my mama's food is so deeply rooted in me that learning how to prepare it was a foregone conclusion. The recipes here are meant to honor my mama, who will forever remain alive in my heart and soul, and most definitely in my kitchen.

SUNNY-SIDE-UP EGGS WITH TOAST

→ **This is perhaps the simplest recipe** in this cookbook yet so essential to my life that I couldn't *not* include it. I've been eating my eggs this way since I was 4, and this continues to be my preferred breakfast. My mama would butter 2 slices of Mrs. Baird's extra-thin white bread and toast it, but I added a little sophistication by using French baguette slices instead. The Maggi sauce is a must—no substitutions, not even soy sauce (as I permit in Sticky Rice with Honey-Glazed Chicken and Chinese Sausage, page 61). Though it seems so simple, there's a complex umami in the Maggi sauce that so perfectly complements the runny egg yolks. I mop up the runny yolk and Maggi sauce with the crust of a baguette slice. Mmmmmm. As a child, I always had a glass of either orange juice or whole milk with this. Nowadays, I like it with a glass of almond milk or Chicory Iced Coffee (page 166).

SERVES 1

1 tablespoon butter

2 (¾-inch-thick) baguette slices

2 large eggs

Maggi sauce

Turn on the broiler and position the oven rack in the middle of the oven. Spread ¼ tablespoon of the butter on each baguette slice, place them on a baking sheet, and lightly toast them on both sides.

In a small nonstick skillet over medium-low heat, melt the remaining ½ tablespoon butter. Swirl to evenly coat the bottom of the pan. Do not let the butter foam; if it does, reduce the heat.

Crack the eggs into the pan and cook them until the whites are opaque and cooked through, 3 to 5 minutes, using a spatula to break up the coagulated whites occasionally so they cook quicker.

With a spatula, slide the eggs onto a plate. Top with a few dashes of Maggi sauce. Serve with the toasted baguette slices.

EGGY OPTIONS

To turn this into a simple rustic lunch, I scramble the eggs and eat them over jasmine rice with a few dashes of Maggi sauce. This method of frying a sunny-side-up egg can also be used when making Bombay Flatbread (page 12).

STIR-FRIED MACARONI WITH BEEF
Nui Xào Bò

✧ **Called *nui* for short,** this is another food from my childhood that evokes true comfort. Like sticky rice with Chinese sausage (see my version on page 61), nui is another recipe my mother turned to when she was short on time but long on love. I just love the effortless, 1-bowl experience this stir-fried macaroni offers: the savory beef, sweet and tangy tomato paste, heat of the garlic, and umami of the Maggi sauce, all mixed in with the jaunty macaroni noodles. It's perfect for kids!

For years, I asked around for this recipe—"you know, the macaroni dish called nui that had garlic and meat and a thin layer of something like tomato paste all mixed in?"—but none of my aunts or friends could tell me exactly how to make it the way I remember my mama making it. I could only do one thing: learn to make it myself. Now every time I eat this dish, I revert to that 9-year-old in our kitchen with the peach-patterned wallpaper and beige linoleum, sitting on a stool with a big bowl of nui in front of me. My mama, dressed in her apron with the cartoon moose on the bib, is still at the stove. She is tasting the macaroni. I am spooning it into my mouth. And together, we are happy.

While many cooks might frown at shocking pasta under cold water, it's essential here so that the pasta doesn't continue to cook; it must be chilled a bit so that it doesn't come apart in the stir-fry.

SERVES 6

1 package (16 ounces) elbow macaroni

½ pound ground beef

½ onion, chopped

2 cloves garlic, minced

Salt and freshly ground black pepper

1 tablespoon tomato paste plus additional, if needed

1 teaspoon Maggi sauce

In a large pot, cook the macaroni according to package directions until al dente. Drain and rinse under cold water.

Heat a wok over medium-high heat. Cook the beef, onion, garlic, and salt and pepper to taste until the meat is browned. Drain the excess fat.

Add the macaroni, 1 tablespoon tomato paste, and Maggi sauce and mix well. The macaroni should be thinly coated in tomato paste; add more tomato paste if necessary. Serve warm.

SUBSTITUTES, AS YOU PLEASE

Ground turkey, ground pork, or even slices of flank or top round beef (always cut across the grain) can be substituted for the ground beef. In a pinch, soy sauce can be used instead of Maggi sauce—but in an authentic Vietnamese kitchen, there's always a bottle of Maggi next to the fish sauce.

GREEN PAPAYA SALAD
Gỏi Đu Đủ Xanh

✧ **A most refreshing salad,** gỏi was a dish present at every special occasion of my youth. Whether it was a Tet—or Lunar New Year—celebration or a memorial dinner in honor of my great-grandparents, my mama and aunts would make this salad with green papaya and sometimes cucumbers, celery, and carrots. At wedding reception banquets (including my own), it is typically served with duck or lobster and lotus root.

In preparing this salad as the first course for the *MasterChef* Season 3 finale, I decided to add the jicama and daikon and use a Japanese spiral turner, which spins vegetables into linguine-like strips. The recipe presented here is the version I made for the show, minus the crab. You can, of course, dress it up with shrimp, pork, chicken, or even cured pork. My favorite way to eat it, however, is simply with shrimp crackers: The idea is to pile a little salad on top of the cracker and pop the whole thing in your mouth. As in all Vietnámese foods, it's all about the perfect balance of textures and flavors.

SERVES 6

FOR THE DRESSING

- 1/2 teaspoon shrimp paste
- 3 tablespoons fish sauce
- 2 tablespoons light olive oil
- Juice of 2 limes
- 1 tablespoon honey

FOR THE SALAD

- 1 carrot, peeled and sliced on the thinnest setting on a mandoline
- 1 jicama, peeled and sliced on the thinnest setting on a mandoline
- 1/2 green papaya, peeled, seeded, and sliced on the thinnest setting on a mandoline
- 1 daikon radish, peeled
- 2 cucumbers, peeled
- 2 red chile peppers, seeded and finely chopped (wear plastic gloves when handling)

FOR THE CANDIED PEANUTS

- 1/2 cup peanuts
- 2 tablespoons palm sugar

TO MAKE THE DRESSING: In a small bowl, whisk together the shrimp paste, fish sauce, olive oil, lime juice, and honey. Cover and refrigerate.

TO MAKE THE SALAD: In a strainer, set the carrot, jicama, and papaya to drain off excess water. Run the radish and cucumbers through a Japanese spiral turner. Alternatively, slice them on the thinnest setting on the mandoline. Drain any excess water.

TO MAKE THE CANDIED PEANUTS: In a small skillet over high heat, combine the peanuts and palm sugar. When the sugar has melted, shake the skillet to coat the peanuts all over. Remove from the heat and set aside to let the sugar harden. When cool, place the peanuts in the bowl of a food processor and pulse 2 to 3 times to coarsely chop. Set aside.

TO SERVE: In a large bowl or on a rimmed serving platter, combine the carrot, jicama, papaya, radish, and cucumbers. Add the chile peppers and toss to combine. Drizzle the dressing over the salad and toss to thoroughly coat. Scatter the peanuts over the salad and serve.

SHRIMP TALK

Shrimp crackers, or *bánh phồng tôm* in Vietnamese, are deep-fried crisps made of prawns and starch. Called *krupuk udang* in their Indonesian land of origin, shrimp crackers are a common snack found in Southeast Asian cuisines. I love letting the cracker stick to my tongue as it gives off a mild pinching sensation that has never been replicated by anything else I've eaten. Although fried, they are light, airy puffs with just the right amount of shrimp flavor. You can buy them already fried: Just tear open the bag and eat.

The dressing for this salad uses shrimp paste, a thick sauce made of fermented ground shrimp. Most people can't stand the smell of this stuff, but as I grew up with it in my foods, I am somewhere between ambivalent about it and enraptured with it. Yes, shrimp paste reeks worse than fish sauce, but if you can get over the aroma, you'll find that a little of it goes a very long way, adding depth to many soups, sauces, curries, and, as in this case, dressings. If, however, you find you can't come around to it, use the Fish Sauce Vinaigrette (page 178), instead of the dressing here.

STICKY RICE WITH HONEY-GLAZED CHICKEN AND CHINESE SAUSAGE
Xôi Gà Mật Ong Lạp Xưởng

Xôi lạp xưởng—or sticky rice with Chinese sausage—is another one of my child-hood favorites. Perfect for weekday meals, it's one of those dishes that my mama would make when she was short on time and energy. Many summer days I'd wake up alone in the house, both parents gone to work, to find a plate of xôi lạp xưởng covered in plastic wrap left for me on the dining table with a note from Mom telling me not to forget the Maggi sauce. In my own version of this recipe, I added nuggets of honey-glazed chicken. This dish is best when you get a little bit of everything in each bite: glutinous rice with a crunchy peanut or two; a slice of salty, crispy Chinese sausage; a little bit of sweet chicken and scallion; and an umami dash of Maggi sauce. Nothing could ever replace time spent with my hardworking mother, but this dish helped ease the longing better than any.

SERVES 6

1½ cups uncooked sweet or glutinous rice (xôi)

⅓ cup raw peanuts

2 tablespoons extra-light olive oil

3 scallions, finely chopped

1 large shallot, finely chopped

4 sticks Chinese sausage, sliced on the diagonal into ¼-inch-thick pieces

6 boneless, skinless chicken thighs, cut into 1-inch pieces

1 tablespoon honey

1 tablespoon brown sugar

Salt and freshly ground black pepper

Maggi sauce

In a rice cooker, steam the rice with the peanuts. Alternatively, cook the rice and peanuts on the stovetop according to the rice package directions.

In a large skillet over medium-high heat, heat the oil. Add the scallions and shallots, reduce the heat to medium-low, and cook, stirring frequently, for 5 minutes or until tender. Transfer to a bowl and set aside.

In the same skillet, over medium heat, pan fry the sausage, stirring frequently, until slightly crispy on the edges. Using tongs or a slotted spoon, transfer the sausage to a second bowl, leaving all the fat in the pan.

Add the chicken, honey, and sugar to the skillet and cook, turning frequently, for 15 minutes or until the meat is no longer pink. Add salt and pepper to taste.

To serve, spoon the sticky rice into 6 bowls. Spoon the sausage and chicken over it and garnish with the scallion and shallot mixture. Serve with Maggi sauce.

WHAT'S XÔI?

From the sweet to the savory, a variety of xôi exists in Vietnamese cuisine. A short-grained, sticky, glutinous rice, xôi is often sold in Vietnam by street vendors for breakfast or as a snack. The xôi used in this recipe is a more savory kind, steamed with peanuts for extra crunch. You can find this particular grain in Chinese or Vietnamese grocery stores labeled as "sweet rice" or "glutinous rice."

AND CHINESE SAUSAGE?

As with xôi, there are also many different forms of Chinese sausage. The kind common in Vietnamese cuisine is lạp xưởng, a hard, dry sausage with a high fat content commonly made of pork. Most lạp xưởng is seasoned with rice wine, soy sauce, and rose water before it's smoked to create sweet undertones. You'll find Chinese sausage in vacuum-sealed packages in Asian food markets.

BRAISED PORK BELLY WITH EGG
Thịt Kho Trứng

↦ **Thịt kho trứng is the quintessential comfort food** of my youth. This was a dish my mama cooked at least once a month. The ingredient list is short, the items simple and inexpensive. And yet the flavors are savory and delectable. I never realized how much I loved this dish until I was older and found myself deeply missing my mama's cooking. As a tribute to her, this was the dish I cooked for my initial *MasterChef* casting call in Austin, and it was also the dish I cooked for the judges at the finale. It was my homage to her cooking, her spirit, and her life. My *MasterChef* journey came full circle.

SERVES 6

2½ pounds pork belly

2 tablespoons vegetable oil

Freshly ground black pepper

2 cans (12 ounces) coconut soda

¼ cup fish sauce plus additional, if desired

¼ cup sugar plus additional, if desired

3 cloves garlic, minced

2 shallots, thinly sliced

1 medium yellow onion, finely chopped

6 hard-boiled eggs, peeled

Chopped scallions

3 cups cooked jasmine rice

In a large saucepan, bring to a boil enough water to cover the pork belly. Add the pork and boil for 3 to 4 minutes. Drain. Rinse the pork belly and wipe out the saucepan. Cut the pork belly into 1-inch pieces and set aside.

In the same saucepan, over medium-high heat, heat the oil. Return the pork to the pan and cook, stirring frequently, until the meat is browned. Transfer the pork to a clay pot and season it with the pepper. Add the coconut soda, ¼ cup fish sauce, ¼ cup sugar, garlic, shallots, onion, and eggs. The liquid should cover both the pork and the eggs; add water if necessary. Bring to a boil on the stove top.

Reduce the heat to low and cover. Braise for 1 to 1½ hours, until the pork is cooked to the desired tenderness. Before serving, adjust the seasoning, adding fish sauce or sugar if necessary, and season again with black pepper. Garnish with the scallions and serve with steamed jasmine rice.

BRAISED PORK RIBLETS
Suòn Kho

✧ **I'm embarrassed to admit it,** but I love gnawing on bones. It doesn't matter if it's a chicken leg, a baby back rib, a sparerib—I have no prejudice. Meat near the bones tends to be juicier, and there's often some ligament, cartilage, and connective tissue for texture. I love this recipe because the ribs are cut down to a manageable size that lets me stuff an entire one in my mouth and, with some expert maneuvering of teeth and tongue, suck the bone dry! Ask your butcher to cut the ribs into 1½-inch pieces for you.

SERVES 4

2 pounds pork ribs, cut crosswise into 1½-inch pieces

2 shallots, finely chopped

2 cloves garlic, minced

1 teaspoon peeled, minced fresh ginger

2 tablespoons fish sauce plus additional, if needed

Salt and freshly ground black pepper

1 tablespoon extra-light olive oil

1 teaspoon sugar plus additional, if needed

1 can (12 ounces) coconut soda

2 scallions, coarsely chopped

In a medium bowl, combine the riblets with the shallots, garlic, ginger, 2 tablespoons fish sauce, and salt and pepper to taste. Cover and refrigerate to marinate for at least 1 hour.

In a large skillet over medium-high heat, heat the oil. Add the 1 teaspoon sugar and stir until it is melted and browned. Toss in the riblets and turn to coat them evenly. Transfer the ribs and sauce to a clay pot.

Add the coconut soda and, if necessary, enough water to cover the meat. Over medium-high heat, bring the liquid to a boil on the stove top and then simmer, covered, until the riblets have absorbed most of the liquid, 60 to 90 minutes. Stir in the scallions during the last 5 minutes of cooking. Taste and adjust the seasonings, adding sugar for more sweetness and fish sauce for more saltiness.

THE ESSENTIAL SECRET INGREDIENT

Coconut soda caramelizes the meat during braising. It does so with more complex flavors than if you were to use sugar and water. The brand of coconut soda I prefer is Coco-Rico. My mama used to have stacks of these 6-packs stored in our pantry, and I never knew what they were used for until years later, when I attempted to make my own thịt kho trứng. I've tried other coconut sodas when I couldn't find Coco-Rico, but the pork never turned out as well—other sodas tend to be too sweet. If you can't get your hands on Coco-Rico, taste the coconut soda first and adjust the amount of sugar in the recipe to your taste. Make sure the label says "coconut soda"—not "coconut milk," "coconut water," or "coconut juice." In a pinch, a can of Coca-Cola Classic can also be substituted.

CLASSIC VERSUS QUICK BRAISING

A clay pot is not a necessity, but the earthenware helps with the caramelization process. You can also use a pressure cooker if you want to cut the cooking time to about a third. Just place all the ingredients in the pressure cooker and cook at 15 pounds per square inch (psi) for approximately 45 minutes. That's what I did for the *MasterChef* Season 3 finale, and it was the dish that helped me gain an edge on my way to a victory.

KEEP YOUR OPTIONS OPEN

To trim the fat, you can discard the skin and fat from the pork belly. Or skip pork belly altogether and use pork butt instead. You'll still get tender pieces of meat, but with less fat. If using pork butt, you can also skip the initial hard-boiling process. Vietnamese braised pork belly is customarily cooked with hard-boiled chicken eggs. For the *MasterChef* Season 3 finale, I wanted to dress up the homey dish a little by pairing it instead with a fried quail egg. This dish is also almost always served with something pickled, to cut the fat. For the finale, I served it with pickled shallots. Either way, it's pure bliss.

MY MAMA'S EGG ROLLS
Chả Giò của Mẹ

✧ **Vietnamese egg rolls** are one of my absolute favorite things to eat—I could easily eat them every day. *Nobody* made them better than my own mama, who would set aside a whole day to make them. Because prepping and cooking them was so time consuming, egg rolls were a rare treat in my home. I liked to help my mama mix the filling, breathing in the pungent aromas of garlic and fish sauce. I loved peeling the egg roll skins apart, and eventually, when I proved to be pretty good at it, she let me try my own hand at wrapping. I've relied on my olfactory and tactile memories to re-create those rolls here. Serve these with Fish Sauce Vinaigrette (page 178), for dipping, or do as I do and eat them straight.

MAKES 50 LARGE OR 100 SMALL EGG ROLLS

4 ounces dried wood ear mushrooms

8 ounces dried bean thread noodles

1 pound ground pork

½ pound shrimp, peeled and minced

1 medium yellow onion, finely chopped

1 large carrot, finely chopped

3 cloves garlic, minced

2 shallots, finely chopped

⅓ cup fish sauce

2 large eggs

Freshly ground black pepper

100 (5 x 5–inch) Filipino egg roll wrappers*

1 egg, beaten

Peanut or canola oil

*Filipino egg roll wrappers are not easy to find. If you can't find them, use rice paper wrappers instead. See "Skin Deep."

Soak the mushrooms and noodles in hot water for 5 to 10 minutes or until tender, then finely chop.

In a large bowl, combine the pork, shrimp, onion, carrot, mushrooms, noodles, garlic, shallots, fish sauce, and eggs and season with pepper to taste. Mix well. Cover and refrigerate for at least 1 hour.

Place a wrapper in front of you with 1 point facing you. Place 1 tablespoon of the filling on the center bottom third of the wrapper, depending on its size.

Fold the bottom corner up over the filling, pinching the skin tightly around the filling to get rid of air pockets. Fold the left corner over the filling, followed by the right. Dab a little beaten egg on the top and roll the egg roll away from you and seal it.

Pour 2 inches of oil into a heavy-bottom saucepan. Heat the oil to 350°F and deep-fry the egg rolls in batches until golden brown and crisp, turning occasionally, making sure not to overcrowd the pan so that they don't stick together.

SKIN DEEP

When shopping for the egg roll skins, try to buy the Filipino wrappers and not the Chinese ones, which are too thick and will produce a bubbly skin after frying. My grandma made even more traditional egg rolls by using Vietnamese rice paper instead of the Filipino skins; if using rice paper, soak the dehydrated rice paper in very hot water to make it pliable before wrapping. Since the rice paper is already sticky, you won't need any egg to seal it.

MY LAST MEAL
The Third Course

There's no question as to what I would want for my third course. My mama's egg rolls are one of the few foods that I can eat for a week straight—at every meal—and not get tired of them. It is pretty typical for me to make this recipe and eat all 100 of them by myself! I know that I loved my mama's egg rolls more than anyone else possibly could, because I had the pleasure of watching her make them. They were a foregone conclusion on birthdays and for potlucks, but my most vivid memories of them were when she made them as a special treat for me on no particular occasion. She'd make the filling the night before, let it marinate in the refrigerator, and then get started early the next morning, rolling, filling, and frying. To this day, the smell of egg rolls sizzling in the fryer makes my stomach growl!

One of my fondest memories of her signature dish was at my fifth-grade celebration of International Day. My mama prepared these egg rolls using ground turkey instead of pork so that my Muslim classmates could eat them, and they were a hit. There were Chinese dumplings, Polish sausages with sauerkraut, and Mexican churros among the multicultural dishes at the meal, but her egg rolls were the first to disappear. I like to think it's because not only was she a great cook, but that she made everything with love. Her egg rolls are always perfect for parties and potlucks—just be sure to stash some away for yourself, or you risk them flying off the platter into hungry mouths.

(For the Fourth Course, see page 95.)

GRILLED BEEF SHORT RIBS
Galbi

✧ **My mama-in-law cooks *galbi* for every birthday dinner** and serves it along with rice and kimchi, Korean spicy pickled cabbage.

Some of the best galbi I've ever had is in LA's Koreatown, where the meat is grilled at the center of the table by a full-service waitstaff. After the beef is nice and charred, the server cuts the ribs into bite-sized pieces with a pair of kitchen shears and drops the morsels of meat straight into your waiting bowl. Now, that's what I call fine dining.

SERVES 4

¾ cup light soy sauce

2 tablespoons packed brown sugar

2 tablespoons sesame oil

1 tablespoon plus 2 teaspoons extra-light olive oil

4 cloves garlic, crushed

3 scallions, white and light green parts only, chopped, plus additional for garnish

2 pounds Korean-style short ribs, thinly cut across the bone

Toasted sesame seeds

In a medium bowl, combine the soy sauce, sugar, sesame oil, olive oil, garlic, and 3 chopped scallions and mix well. Place the ribs into two large resealable plastic bags and divide the soy sauce mixture between them. Shake to evenly distribute the marinade. Refrigerate overnight. Turn the bags over once as the beef marinates.

Heat a grill or grill pan to medium-high heat. Drain the excess marinade off the meat, scrape away the scallions, and grill for 6 to 8 minutes, turning once. Garnish the ribs with additional chopped scallions and the toasted sesame seeds and serve.

WHAT IS FLANKEN?

Called the flanken cut, Korean-style short ribs are sliced thinly across the bone toward the chuck end of the ribs. The result is a strip of meat roughly 8 inches long and ½ inch thick with 3 or 4 cross-sectioned bones on each slice. This thin cut makes the rib meat ideal for grilling. You can ask the butcher to prepare the short ribs with a flanken cut, or find them presliced at Korean markets.

CLAY POT CATFISH
Cá Kho Tộ

◇ **I made this for Gordon Ramsay,** Graham Elliot, and Joe Bastianich during my *MasterChef* Season 3 audition because (1) it represents my heritage, (2) it can be cooked in less than an hour, and (3) it's damn delicious. I served it with Quick Pickled Cucumbers and Carrots (page 141), which earned me a white apron and a spot in the top 36. The rest, as you know, is history.

The quintessentially humble peasant food of Vietnam, this dish takes what many consider a lowbrow fish and employs a braising technique that brings out the best in its sweet, tender flesh. The steaks are first seared and then cooked low and slow in a clay pot for optimum caramelization.

Cá kho tộ is one of those quotidian dishes at the center of many family meals. I recall eating the succulent fish throughout my youth. My mama would comb the fish, looking for every splinter of bone before dropping the bite-size nuggets into my bowl. I loved the sweet and savory sauce and always asked for an extra pour over my rice. Serve this with Sour Prawn Soup (page 44) for a perfect balance of flavors.

SERVES 4

¼ cup canola oil

2 small shallots, sliced

2 cloves garlic, minced

1 teaspoon ground red pepper

4 (1–1½-inch-thick) skinless catfish steaks

Savory Caramel Sauce (page 173)

2 tablespoons fish sauce

3 cups steamed jasmine rice

Quick Pickled Cucumbers and Carrots (page 141)

2 scallions, thinly sliced

Cilantro sprigs

Lemon wedges

In a large, heavy-bottom sauté pan over medium-high heat, heat the oil. Cook the shallots and garlic, stirring frequently, for 1 minute or just until fragrant. Stir in the pepper. Add the catfish steaks and cook until they are golden brown on both sides but still raw in the center. Transfer the catfish to a clay pot. (Be sure your clay pot is approved for stove-top cooking.) Pour off the oil from the pan and spoon the shallots and garlic over the fish in the pot.

Pour the Savory Caramel Sauce over the fish in the pot. Add the fish sauce and simmer, uncovered, over medium heat for 15 minutes or until reduced by half.

Mound the steamed rice in 4 wide bowls. Set the catfish steaks on top of the rice and spoon the sauce over the fish. Set the bowls on large plates. Mound the Quick Pickled Cucumbers and Carrots on the plates. Sprinkle the scallions over the fish and pickles and garnish with the cilantro. Serve immediately with the lemon wedges.

WHERE'D YOU GET THAT LOVELY CATFISH?

Catfish steaks can be challenging to find. I suggest going to a fishmonger or an Asian specialty market where catfish is sold whole, then asking the fishmonger to cut it up into steaks. I prefer that the skin also be removed, as I find it a bit oily. The fishmonger may discard the head and tail, but you may want to ask for them; the head and tail make a nice substitute for prawns in Sour Prawn Soup (page 44).

Chapter 4

Western Classics

I am Vietnamese by heritage but American in practically every other way. I was born in sunny Southern California and raised in Houston, Texas. From grade school all the way up to college, I ate cafeteria food. It was in those institutions, fast-food joints, diners, and the homes of friends that I was introduced to American comfort food.

While Vietnamese food is among my favorite cuisines today, growing up, it was always food from other places that piqued my interest. Like many children, I took what I had at home for granted and constantly yearned for what my friends were eating. At the school lunch table, I'd trade one of my mama's egg rolls for a bite of a classmate's spaghetti. It didn't matter that it was noodles and fake tomatoes from a can—it was something I didn't get often, and it was both intriguing and tasty.

Every Wednesday was hamburger day on the school lunch menu, and I begged my mama for the dollar and 10 cents it cost for hot lunch. During my freshman year in high school, when I was finally allowed to start making my own food choices at the supermarket, I discovered personal-sized chicken pot pies in the freezer section. It was at a friend's house my junior year that I had my first bite of meat loaf—we ate it straight out of the Tupperware container, not bothering to heat it up, and it was delicious.

Fried chicken is perhaps one of the few American comfort foods that I actually *did* get at home (albeit bought and not made by my parents). I'm not sure if it's because it was permitted by my parents or simply because it just tastes *so good*, but to this day, southern fried chicken remains one of my favorite foods. This chapter is full of the foods I discovered beyond my mother's kitchen, the dishes that satiated both my curiosity and my appetite. Chicken Pot Pie, Pulled Pork Sandwiches, super-juicy burgers—what was not to love? It didn't take me very long to embrace these classics, and today, I'm all the better a cook for it. My kitchen is a multicultural one, and it doesn't get more American than that.

PENNE WITH VODKA SAUCE

✧ **I made this dish** for a small group of friends for their collective birthdays, and it was a big hit. The best part is they don't know how quick and easy it was to prepare.

I tend to gravitate toward penne, or any bite-sized pasta for that matter, because I find it so much easier to eat—jab a fork in it, place in mouth, and chew. No slurping or twirling as with linguine, no messy sauce dripping from your chin. Tidiness is obviously a challenge for any blind person, so I like to take the guesswork out of the eating equation and just go with the simpler pastas, like rotini, fusilli, or penne.

SERVES 6

8 Roma tomatoes, peeled
(see "Score, Blanch, Peel" on page 34)

1 tablespoon plus 2 teaspoons
extra-virgin olive oil

3 strips pancetta, cut into 1-inch pieces

6 ounces Italian sausage, casings removed

3 cloves garlic, minced

1 medium yellow onion, finely chopped

½ teaspoon crushed red-pepper flakes

Salt

1 package (16 ounces) penne

1 tablespoon plus 2 teaspoons vodka

¼ cup heavy cream

2 tablespoons chopped fresh basil (optional)

Parmesan (optional)

A FORGIVING DISH

For a lower-fat alternative, use half-and-half instead of heavy cream. If you find yourself short of time, you can substitute 1½ (14.5-ounce) cans of crushed tomatoes for the fresh tomatoes. And if you want to make this vegetarian, leave out the pancetta and sausage and add some slices of portobello mushrooms and spinach.

Cut each tomato in half, discard the seeds, and squeeze the tomatoes dry. In the bowl of a food processor, finely chop the tomatoes.

In a medium saucepan over medium heat, heat the oil. Cook the pancetta and sausage until browned, breaking up the sausage with a wooden spoon. Add the garlic, onion, and red-pepper flakes and cook, stirring frequently, 5 minutes longer or until the onions are soft and fragrant. Add the tomatoes and salt to taste. Raise the heat and bring the sauce to a boil, then reduce the heat and simmer for 15 minutes.

Cook the penne according to package directions or until al dente. Drain and set aside.

Add the vodka and cream and bring the sauce to a low boil. Toss the sauce with the pasta and serve garnished with the basil and Parmesan, if desired.

PASTA 101

Dried pasta should always be cooked al dente, which means "to the tooth" in Italian. Al dente refers to the doneness of the pasta: When bitten, it should have a firm resistance; if it's too soft, it's overcooked, and if it's hard in the center, it's undercooked. Here are a few tips to get perfect al dente pasta every time:

1. Use plenty of water: One pound (16 ounces) of pasta should cook in 4 to 6 quarts of water.
2. Start with cold water and add salt only after the water has started boiling.
3. Don't add the dried pasta until the water is at a rolling boil.
4. Begin checking the pasta by biting into it after 4 minutes.
5. Toss the pasta immediately with the sauce and serve.

Americans tend to oversauce their pasta. Do as the Italians do and use a smaller sauce-to-pasta ratio. Or, if you really want to take the phrase "when in Rome" to the next level, make your own pasta from scratch. But that's a lesson for a whole other cookbook.

SPAGHETTI AND MEATBALLS

I've eaten a lot of spaghetti and meatballs in my lifetime. I've had the kind straight out of a can. I've had it from the frozen cardboard box. I've had it on a Styrofoam school lunch tray. I've had it with sauce from a jar. I've never had it, however, cooked by an Italian-American grandma, so I decided to do as I've always done: I learned to make it myself.

SERVES 6

1 pound ground beef

1 cup bread crumbs

1 clove garlic, minced

1 tablespoon parsley

1 tablespoon grated Parmesan plus additional, if desired

1 tablespoon grated Asiago cheese

1/4 teaspoon freshly ground black pepper

1 large egg, beaten

Perfect Spaghetti Sauce (page 83)

1 package (16 ounces) spaghetti

Preheat the oven to 350°F. Coat a baking sheet with a thin layer of oil. In a large bowl, combine the beef, bread crumbs, garlic, parsley, 1 tablespoon Parmesan, Asiago, pepper, and egg and mix thoroughly but gently with your hands. Shape by the tablespoonful into meatballs and place on the baking sheet, leaving a 1/2-inch space between them. Bake until the outsides of the meatballs have entirely lost their pink color, 20 to 25 minutes.

In a large pot over medium-high heat, simmer the meatballs in the Perfect Spaghetti Sauce for 30 minutes.

Meanwhile, in a large pot of water, cook the spaghetti according to package directions or until al dente (see "Pasta 101" on page 81). Drain. Ladle the meatballs and sauce over the spaghetti and sprinkle with additional Parmesan, if desired.

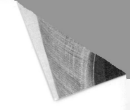

PERFECT SPAGHETTI SAUCE

MAKES 1½ to 2 QUARTS

24 Roma tomatoes, peeled (see "Score, Blanch, Peel" on page 34) or 2 cans (28 ounces each) crushed tomatoes

¼ cup extra-virgin olive oil

1 medium yellow onion, chopped

4 cloves garlic, minced

2 teaspoons salt

½ teaspoon freshly ground black pepper

1 teaspoon sugar

1 can (6 ounces) tomato paste

1 teaspoon dried basil

1 teaspoon dried oregano

Cut each tomato in half, discard the seeds, and squeeze the tomatoes dry. In the bowl of a food processor, finely chop the tomatoes.

In a large saucepan over medium heat, heat the oil. Cook the onion and garlic, stirring frequently, until soft and fragrant. Stir in the tomatoes, salt, pepper, and sugar. Cover, reduce the heat to low, and simmer for 1 hour 30 minutes or until the tomatoes have completely broken down. Add the tomato paste, basil, and oregano to the tomato sauce (and meatballs if making Spaghetti and Meatballs). Simmer for 30 minutes longer.

BAKED ZITI

One of my favorite TV shows of all time is *The Sopranos*, and part of the reason (besides the awesome acting and riveting plot lines) is because the characters were always eating so well. I watched the series when I still had vision, and every time I saw them gather around a table to eat, my mouth would water.

Baked ziti was one of those homey comfort foods Carmela Soprano cooked for her family, freezing it for when her husband had a hankering and delivering it to their daughter who was away at college. Because everyone loved Carmela's baked ziti, it became something I wanted to learn to prepare myself.

This ziti was one of the first dishes I made when my affinity for cooking began, and because it's simple and tasty, it's still a part of my repertoire. The great thing about baked pasta is exactly what Carmela demonstrated: You can freeze it and bake it whenever a craving hits. To make a vegetarian version, simply omit the sausage.

SERVES 6 TO 8

1 package (16 ounces) ziti

1 pound Italian sausage, casings removed

4 cloves garlic, minced

1 medium yellow onion, finely chopped

Perfect Spaghetti Sauce (page 83)

½ bunch spinach, coarsely chopped

1 cup sour cream

12 slices provolone cheese

1½ cups (6 ounces) freshly grated mozzarella cheese

½ cup (2 ounces) freshly grated Parmesan

¼–½ cup chopped fresh basil

In a large pot of water, cook the ziti according to package directions until slightly firmer than al dente.

In a medium saucepan over medium heat, brown the sausage. Add the garlic and onion and cook, stirring frequently, for 5 minutes or until fragrant and soft. Drain the fat from the pan. Stir in the spaghetti sauce and spinach and simmer for 15 minutes or until the spinach is wilted and the sauce is heated through. Stir in the sour cream and set aside.

Preheat the oven to 350°F. Lightly grease a 2-quart baking dish. Arrange half of the ziti in the dish, then top with a layer of half the provolone and half the mozzarella. Pour half of the spaghetti sauce over, pushing the sauce out to the edges of the dish. Cover with the remaining pasta, provolone, mozzarella, and sauce. Sprinkle the Parmesan over and bake until the cheese is bubbling and golden, 30 to 40 minutes. Garnish with the basil and serve.

PASTA 102

When preparing pasta that is cooked twice, as in Baked Ziti, the pasta should be cooked slightly less than al dente in the first cooking. Prepare according to package directions, but shave the cooking time by one-third. The pasta should be pliable but not fully cooked.

CKEN POT PIE

✧ **The first chicken pot pie** I ever had came in a cardboard box from the frozen food section of a grocery store. Years later, after a certain Thanksgiving left me with almost a pound of uneaten turkey, I decided to try my own hand at a turkey pot pie. Temperatures outside were near freezing that day, and fragrant buttery crust, herb-scented turkey, and vegetable filling made home the only place I wanted to be that evening. There's nothing more comforting than breaking through the flaky crust and pulling out tender, juicy nuggets bathed in a soothing, creamy sauce. Of course, leftover chicken is a more common occurrence in my house, so when I find myself with more than a cup of it, I make an entire meal from it in this pot pie.

SERVES 8

1 Flaky Pie Crust (page 157)

3 tablespoons butter

1 small yellow onion, minced

2 stalks celery, coarsely chopped

2 medium carrots, diced

2 tablespoons dried parsley

2 teaspoons dried thyme

1/2 teaspoon dried oregano

Salt and freshly ground black pepper

1 3/4 cups Poultry Stock (page 172) or low-sodium chicken broth

1 large Yukon Gold potato, cut into 1-inch cubes

2 tablespoons flour

1/2 cup milk

12 ounces cooked chicken, cubed

2 teaspoons melted butter, for brushing the crust

Roll out half of the pie crust to 1/4-inch thickness. Lay the dough in a 9-inch pie pan.

In a large sauté pan over medium heat, melt 1 1/2 tablespoons of the butter. Add the onion, celery, carrots, parsley, thyme, and oregano. Season with the salt and pepper. Cover and cook for 10 minutes, stirring occasionally, or until the vegetables are tender. Add the stock to the pan, raise the heat, and bring to a boil. Add the potato, cover, and cook for 10 to 12 minutes, or until the potato is tender but still firm.

In a medium saucepan over medium-high heat, melt the remaining 1 1/2 tablespoons butter. Stir in the flour, whisking until it is free of lumps. Add the milk and chicken and bring to a low boil. Transfer the chicken mixture to the vegetable mixture and cook, uncovered, for 20 minutes, or until the liquid is thick enough to coat the back of a spoon.

Preheat the oven to 425°F. Pour the filling into the pie pan. Roll out the remaining pie dough to 1/4-inch thickness and drape it over the filling. Trim the overhanging dough, then flute the edges to seal the crusts together. Brush the melted butter over the top crust. Using a very sharp knife, make 4 slits in the top of the pie for steam to escape.

Bake for 15 minutes, then reduce the heat to 350°F and bake for 35 minutes longer, or until the crust is golden. Serve warm.

FRESH VERSUS DRIED: WHICH HERBS DO YOU USE? AND WHEN?

Fresh herbs are always lovely to incorporate into your dishes. But in the case of Chicken Pot Pie, you want the flavors of the herbs to thoroughly permeate the pie filling as it bakes, which is better achieved with dried herbs. A general rule of thumb is that dried herbs should be added before or during the cooking process, while fresh herbs are best added at the end, as a garnish. When fresh herbs are exposed to heat over a long period of time, they lose their flavor.

BUTTERMILK FRIED CHICKEN

✧ **One of my favorite things in the world** to eat is fried chicken, and when I was growing up in Texas, southern fried chicken was a monthly staple on our family table. I wasn't lucky enough to have a grandma who fried up chicken in a vat of lard. (I *was*, however, lucky enough to have a grandma who fried up egg rolls instead!) No, my childhood fried chicken experience consisted of Popeye's. As with every other classic American comfort food, I had to learn how to make fried chicken through my own trial and error. When I made it on *MasterChef*, I used blood oranges, since I like their sweeter flavor, but you could essentially use any oranges or even orange juice. Buttermilk Fried Chicken goes great with Dirty Rice (page 146), Haricots Verts with Pancetta (page 132), Roasted Brussels Sprouts with Caramelized Fish Sauce (page 136), Cowboy Corn on the Cob (page 139), or Garlic Mashed Potatoes (page 142).

SERVES 4

1½ cups buttermilk

Zest and juice of 2 oranges

1 tablespoon plus 2 teaspoons kosher salt

1 teaspoon freshly ground black pepper

8 chicken drumsticks

Canola oil

1¼ cups all-purpose flour

1¼ cups cornmeal

1 tablespoon plus 1 teaspoon garlic powder

4 teaspoons onion powder

4 teaspoons sweet paprika

½ teaspoon ground red pepper

In a large bowl, whisk the buttermilk, orange zest and juice, 1 tablespoon of the salt, and ½ teaspoon of the black pepper to blend. Add the chicken and turn to coat. Cover and refrigerate for at least 30 minutes and up to 1 day, rotating the drumsticks to marinate evenly.

Position a rack in the center of the oven and preheat the oven to 200°F or the lowest setting. Line a baking sheet with parchment paper or aluminum foil, and set a wire cooling rack on top. In a large, heavy-bottom skillet over medium heat, heat 1½ inches of oil to 350°F.

In a large resealable plastic bag, mix the flour, cornmeal, garlic powder, onion powder, paprika, red pepper, and the remaining 2 teaspoons salt and ½ teaspoon black pepper. Drain the chicken in a colander and discard the marinade. Add the chicken, one piece at a time, to the bag and shake to coat well. Tap off the excess flour mixture and transfer the chicken pieces to a sheet of waxed paper.

Add 4 drumsticks to the hot oil and cook, turning occasionally with tongs, for 10 to 12 minutes or until golden brown and cooked through. Transfer the chicken to the rack and keep it warm in the oven. Return the oil to 350°F before frying the remaining 4 drumsticks.

THE SECRET TO LIGHT AND CRISPY DEEP-FRYING

When deep-frying, be careful not to overcrowd the pot, as this will lower the oil's temperature, resulting in soggy, greasy food. Lay the finished chicken on wire cooling racks over foil or parchment paper, then place the racks in the oven on low heat to keep the chicken warm while you fry the rest of the pieces.

PULLED PORK SANDWICHES

✧ **I wouldn't be a true Texas gal** if I didn't include a barbecue dish in this cookbook.
If you know anything about barbecue, you know that every state and region of the South has its
own version. In the Carolinas, entire hogs are slow-smoked. And in South Carolina, the barbecue
boasts a mustard-heavy sauce. Tennessee has mastered pork ribs and often serves them dry or with
a little bit of tomato and vinegar sauce. The Deep South gravitates toward pork sandwiches. And in
Texas, beef brisket with a sweet sauce is king. While I do love brisket, my heart belongs to pulled
pork. I find it more tender and more readily soaks up the flavors of the marinade.

Full disclosure: Purists may take issue with my Pulled Pork Sandwiches. True barbecue is
slow-cooked outdoors, smoked for hours in an open pit at a low heat over wood chips. I make
mine in the oven.

These Pulled Pork Sandwiches are great for parties, because a 5-pound pork roast is both cheap
and enough to feed a lot of hungry folks. While you have to prepare it a day in advance of cooking
and the next day let it cook for hours, most of the time the work is hands-off, meaning you can
busy yourself with making the Cowboy Corn on the Cob (page 139) to serve on the side. (Or you can
simply tear open a bag of good-quality potato chips.)

SERVES 10

1 boneless pork shoulder roast (5 pounds)

½–¾ cup Barbecue Dry Rub (page 181)

¾ cup Barbecue Sauce (page 175), plus more
for serving

10 hamburger buns, toasted

1 onion, thinly sliced

2 pickles, thinly sliced

Pat the pork dry with paper towels. Rub the
Barbecue Dry Rub generously all over the
pork. Cover with plastic wrap and refrigerate
overnight.

Bring the pork to room temperature for 1 hour.
Preheat the oven to 225°F. Place the pork in a
baking dish, inserting a digital meat thermometer into the thickest part. Roast in the oven for
7 to 8 hours, or until the meat reaches 180°F
and is falling-apart tender. Remove the pork
from the oven and let it rest for 20 minutes.
Using 2 forks, shred it into small pieces and
place them in a large bowl. Add the Barbecue
Sauce and mix until incorporated throughout.

Spoon the pulled pork onto the bottom half of
each bun. Serve open faced with onion, pickles,
and additional barbecue sauce on the side.

MEAT LOAF

✧ **Growing up, I always thought meat loaf** was unappetizing—not because I'd eaten it and formed that opinion myself, but because many Americans I knew scowled at the thought of meat loaf, dismissing it as a dish reserved for when you didn't know what else to do with a bunch of random leftovers in the fridge. It wasn't until high school that I tasted my first bite of meat loaf at a friend's house. That first forkful, dipped in ketchup, made me realize just how delicious this American classic is. Serve it with a side of Garlic Mashed Potatoes (page 142) and Haricots Verts with Pancetta (page 132) and you've got yourself a true American meal.

SERVES 4

1 tablespoon extra-light olive oil

1 large onion, finely chopped

¾ teaspoon fresh thyme leaves

1 teaspoon salt

½ teaspoon freshly ground black pepper

3 tablespoons Worcestershire sauce

¼ cup plus 2 tablespoons beef broth

¼ teaspoon tomato paste

2½ pounds ground beef

¼ cup plain bread crumbs

2 large eggs, beaten

¼ cup plus 2 tablespoons ketchup

Preheat the oven to 350°F. In a medium pan over medium-low heat, heat the oil. Add the onion and thyme and cook, stirring frequently, for 5 minutes or until the onion is fragrant and translucent. Season with the salt and pepper and transfer to a large bowl.

Add the Worcestershire sauce, beef broth, and tomato paste to the onion mixture and mix well. Let cool to room temperature. Add the ground beef, bread crumbs, and eggs and mix well with your hands. Shape the meat into a 2 x 5 x 8-inch loaf and set it in a baking dish. Spread the ketchup evenly over the top. Place a deep pan filled with water on the bottommost rack in the oven. Place the meat loaf on the rack above it. This will prevent the meat loaf from drying out and cracking on the surface. Bake until the meat loaf is cooked through, 30 to 45 minutes. Serve warm.

MEAT LOAF METHODS

Looking for a healthier option? Substitute ground turkey and Poultry Stock (page 172) or low-sodium chicken broth for the beef and beef broth.

MY LAST MEAL
The Fourth Course

I would swing back to my American roots for my fourth course. Pizza would be on the menu. Nothing fancy, just a straight-from-the-oven pizza with a bubbling, crackling New York–style thin crust, the freshest tomato sauce, and creamy mozzarella cheese.

My mama was just as avid a shopper as she was a cook, spending every Saturday at the mall sifting through racks of clothes marked for clearance. I was always dragged along on these shopping trips, but instead of combing the clothes racks, I'd hit the bookstore instead. Sometimes my mama would shop for so long that I'd finished half a novel before she came to fetch me. As a reward for not getting lost or in trouble, she'd buy me a slice of cheese pizza at the food court.

The pizza joint at the mall was run by a pack of Italian brothers who'd relocated from New York in the early '80s, bringing their accents and pizza-making skills to Texas. Because my mama and I were regular customers (yes, we were at the mall that often), they frequently gave us a discount on our orders. I used to dump so much Parmesan on my pizza that it would elicit stares from the surrounding pizza lovers. But I never paid attention. I was sharing one of my favorite foods with my mama, a memory that I will forever cherish.

(For the Fifth Course, see page 147.)

MUSHROOM AND ONION BURGERS

✧ **When my mama was pregnant** with me, she craved hamburgers. She would waddle down the few blocks from my parents' Chicago apartment to a corner diner and order a hamburger. It's no wonder I love them so much. Of course, it doesn't hurt that I live in the land of cattle and cowboy boots!

My favorite burger is a pretty simple one: a well-seasoned, quality beef patty, a slice of melted cheese, and some mushrooms and onions sautéed in butter—all wedged between 2 butter-toasted buns. I prefer to go minimal on the condiments—just a dab of mustard and mayo—and then maybe a bit of arugula and tomato for added spark.

These burgers are great for summer gatherings. You can set up a build-your-own-burger buffet with standard condiments: pickles, ketchup, lettuce, bacon, etc. Or, for a fancier version, dress it up with seared foie gras (or some liver mousse if you live in California), aioli, chipotle raspberry jam, and a fried egg (see Sunny-Side-Up Eggs with Toast, page 56, for how to make the perfect fried egg).

SERVES 4

$2/3$ pound prime ground chuck

$1/3$ pound prime ground sirloin

3 tablespoons bread crumbs

$1/4$ small onion, finely chopped, plus $1/2$ onion, thinly sliced

1 clove garlic, minced

1 teaspoon Worcestershire sauce

1 teaspoon soy sauce

1 large egg

$1/2$ teaspoon salt

$1/4$ teaspoon freshly ground black pepper

3 tablespoons butter

12 button mushrooms, sliced

2 ounces Cheddar cheese, cut into 4 slices

4 hamburger buns topped with sesame seeds

Mayonnaise (optional)

Mustard (optional)

Arugula (optional)

Tomato slices (optional)

In a large bowl, combine the ground chuck and sirloin, bread crumbs, chopped onion, garlic, Worcestershire sauce, soy sauce, egg, salt, and pepper and mix lightly with a fork. (Avoid over-mixing, or the burger will be dry and crumbly; a loose mixture ensures a tender burger.) Using your hands, gently shape the mixture into four 1-inch-thick patties.

In a large skillet over medium-high heat, melt 2 tablespoons of the butter. Add the sliced onion and cook, stirring frequently, for 5 minutes or until tender and fragrant. Add the mushrooms and cook, stirring frequently, until they are browned and tender. Remove from the heat and set aside.

Preheat a grill or grill pan to high heat. Cook the patties for 2 minutes on each side. Reduce the heat and cook for 2 minutes longer on each side. Do not flip the patties again. Place 1 cheese slice on each patty and cook for 1 minute longer or until the cheese melts.

Meanwhile, spread the remaining 1 tablespoon butter on the tops of the 4 buns. Toast the bun tops and bottoms cut side down on the grill for 1 minute or until golden.

To assemble the burgers, spread some mayonnaise, if using, on the bottom half of each bun. Set a patty on top, then top with the mushroom mixture. Serve with the mustard, arugula, and tomato slices on the side, if desired.

TALKING TURKEY

When I'm really watching what I put in my mouth, I opt to use ground turkey rather than beef here. Unlike beef, turkey must be cooked all the way through; grill your turkey burgers on each side for 5 minutes, checking for doneness to determine if they need to spend more time on the grill.

Chapter 5

Food for Casual Gatherings

I came to love entertaining long before I became a good cook. It all began in college when I was learning how to make food for myself. I invited my roommates and friends to the table because I always had extra—there weren't many recipes around that yielded one serving. Sometimes the dishes I prepared were downright inedible, and my friends swore they would never come around to eat again. "Are the carrots supposed to taste like a

fire pit?" they'd tease. "Is the beef supposed to hurt my teeth?" Most of the time, however, the food was average: edible but not particularly exciting. My guests would graciously eat it but shun offers of seconds. Once in a while, though, I would enjoy the sight of plates scraped clean and the satisfied gazes around the table, and it was these rare moments that brought me to the realization that I loved to feed people. I was a natural-born hostess; I just had to learn how to cook!

Fifteen years later, my love for cooking for others has not waned. My kitchen skills have, of course, improved, and now the social gatherings around my dining table vary from formal multicourse meals to casual barbecues. My favorite kind of entertaining, however, coincides with my favorite holiday: Thanksgiving. This is when all the comfort foods come out, calorie counting is ignored, and everyone gets together to raise a glass, share great food, and be in the best company. It has been an annual tradition in our household to throw a day-after-Thanksgiving leftovers potluck in which everyone we know brings a leftover dish from the big feast, and we fry up three whole turkeys for the shindig. A party of this caliber can have its fair share of mishaps. From the slow-to-heat frying oil to the inebriated neighbor to the pinot noir splattered all over the ecru cushion, I've experienced it all under my roof. But no party is perfect, and these will become moments of hilarity to reminisce about in the future. For now, remember that everyone— including you—has gathered around you to have a good time. There's no use crying over spilled wine, so just break out the stain remover, smile, and keep on eating. Learn to improvise and enjoy yourself; that's what entertaining is all about.

TERIYAKI CHICKEN AND PINEAPPLE SKEWERS

✧ **I started hosting barbecues with my friends** when I was in college. Back then, we would pool our money and buy cheap cuts of meat, fruits, and veggies to throw on the fire. We'd grill, eat, swim in the apartment complex pool, dry off, and eat some more. When I think about it, those simpler days were the best ones, in which all that mattered was food and friends (and perhaps a nice tan!).

This is a twist on a simple chicken skewer we made so many years ago; I've given it a Hawaiian flavor by alternating chunks of pineapple with the teriyaki-marinated chicken on the skewers.

SERVES 6

1 tablespoon extra-light olive oil

3 cloves garlic, crushed

¾ teaspoon peeled and crushed fresh ginger

½ cup soy sauce

¼ cup apple cider vinegar

½ cup brown sugar

¼ teaspoon freshly ground black pepper

1 tablespoon cornstarch

1 tablespoon water

12 boneless, skinless chicken thighs, cut into chunks

Kosher salt

1 pineapple, peeled and cut into 1-inch cubes

Soak six 8-inch wooden skewers in water for at least 30 minutes. In a small saucepan over medium-low heat, heat the olive oil. Cook the garlic and ginger, stirring frequently, for 3 minutes or until fragrant. Add the soy sauce, vinegar, brown sugar, and pepper and reduce the heat to low.

In a small bowl, stir the cornstarch into the water. Add the mixture to the saucepan and let simmer, stirring frequently, until the sauce thickens and bubbles. Remove from the heat and cool to room temperature.

In a large bowl, combine the chicken with the teriyaki sauce. Cover and marinate in the refrigerator for at least 1 hour.

Lightly salt the pineapple. Divide the pineapple and chicken among the skewers, threading them in an alternating fashion and shaking off excess marinade from the chicken chunks. Heat a grill pan over medium-high heat until hot. Working in batches if necessary, grill the skewers, turning, for 10 minutes or until the juices run clear when the chicken is pierced with a knife.

SIMPLE SUBSTITUTIONS

This is a very forgiving recipe. Honey may be used in place of the brown sugar, and chicken breasts in place of the chicken thighs. You can even use canned, drained pineapple chunks if you don't have time to chop up a fresh pineapple.

CHICKEN TIKKA MASALA

✧ My college roommate introduced me to Indian food. We lived together in a tiny dorm room our freshman year, and every time she returned from a weekend back home, our mini fridge would fill up with containers of colorful, pungent curries. Whenever she heated up her mama's food in the microwave, the aromas would linger in the hall, causing all the girls on our floor to salivate. My roommate, who was very nurturing by nature, always fed me a bite here and there with the intention of expanding my palate. I must say it wasn't love at first bite—my tongue had trouble handling the spiciness—but after we graduated, I realized I missed her mama's meals. Call it nostalgia for our undergrad days, but I find myself occasionally hankering for those bright, complex flavors.

I learned to make Chicken Tikka Masala after I got fed up with my constant cravings, and I must say it paid off when it came to the food truck Team Challenge on *MasterChef* Season 3. Our team was assigned an Indian theme, which instantly brought back memories of my roommate and those containers. Once we started serving, we even had customers get back in line for seconds, and when our time was up and the challenge was finished, the film crew gobbled up the leftovers. I like to think of this recipe as the one that saved us from the chopping block!

I serve this with basmati rice and *naan* (an Indian flatbread made in a clay oven) to soak up all the saucy goodness. You can find packaged naan in many grocery and specialty stores.

SERVES 4

1 cup plain yogurt

1 tablespoon lemon juice

4 teaspoons ground cumin

1 teaspoon ground red pepper

1 teaspoon freshly ground black pepper

1 tablespoon peeled, minced fresh ginger

1 teaspoon ground cinnamon

Salt

3 boneless, skinless chicken breasts or thighs, cut into 1-inch chunks

2 tablespoons butter

3 cloves garlic, minced

1 tablespoon paprika

1½ cups canned tomato sauce

1½ cups heavy cream

¼ cup chopped cilantro

Soak four 8-inch wooden skewers in water for at least 30 minutes. In a large bowl, combine the yogurt, lemon juice, 2 teaspoons of the cumin, and the red pepper, black pepper, ginger, cinnamon, and salt. Add the chicken and toss to coat. Cover and refrigerate for 1 hour.

In a large saucepan over medium heat, melt the butter. Stir in the garlic and cook, stirring frequently, until fragrant. Add the paprika, additional salt to taste, and the remaining teaspoons cumin. Stir in the tomato sauce and cream. Simmer for 20 minutes, or until the sauce thickens.

Meanwhile, thread the chicken onto the soaked skewers, dividing it evenly. Discard the marinade. Heat a grill pan over medium-high heat until hot. Grill the chicken 5 minutes on each side, or until the juices run clear when the chicken is pierced with a knife. Remove the chicken from the skewers.

Transfer the chicken to the simmering sauce and simmer an additional 10 minutes. Transfer to a serving dish and garnish with the cilantro. Serve with basmati rice and naan.

SPICE IS NICE

Garam masala is a mixture of spices commonly used in Indian cuisine. The exact ingredients vary from region to region and brand to brand; most versions will contain peppercorns, cumin, cinnamon, cloves, and cardamom. You can use it in conjunction with or in place of the spices called for in this recipe.

Like the fire-in-the-hole flavor of extra-spicy food? Go heavier on the ground red pepper here. If too much heat scares you, reduce the amount of red pepper to your liking or omit it altogether.

WHO DOESN'T LOVE OPTIONS?

Occasionally, when I want to minimize cleanup duty, I make this dish without using a grill. Instead of skewering and grilling, I cook the marinated chunks of chicken on the stove top, stirring frequently, until the juices run clear. Then I add the chicken to the tomato cream sauce and finish cooking as directed.

CAJUN FRIED TURKEY

✧ **Once you go fried, you never go dry,** and roasted turkey becomes a thing of Thanksgivings past. I served fried turkey at the first Thanksgiving dinner I dared to host back when I was 22 years old. Living in the South and right next door to Louisiana's Cajun country, I'd been hearing about fried turkey for a while. Being a true Southern gal and loving anything fried, I decided to try my own hand at turkey frying. This method cuts down the cooking time to a mere fraction of the time it takes to roast, which means I don't have to wake up at 6 a.m. to get dinner started. Instead, I can pop open a beer at 5 p.m. and enjoy the mild Houston winter while inhaling the intoxicating aromas of the bird frying on the outdoor propane burner. It may not be the healthiest thing on the Thanksgiving menu, but that's what New Year's resolutions are for!

SERVES 10 TO 12

1 (12-pound) fresh turkey

2 cups Cajun Turkey Marinade (at right)

¼ cup Cajun Seasoning (page 180)

3 gallons peanut oil

One day before cooking, remove the giblets from the turkey and rinse the bird inside and out. Pat it dry with paper towels.

Inject the marinade into the turkey as follows: 1 full food syringe into each leg, 1 into each thigh, half a syringe into each wing, and 2 full syringes into each breast. As you inject the marinade, pull the needle out slowly to allow the marinade to spread evenly throughout the turkey. Rub the inside and outside of the turkey liberally with the seasoning. Refrigerate the turkey overnight.

When ready to cook, fill a 40-quart pot half full with the oil. Set it on a sturdy propane burner and heat it to 400°F or until lines appear in the oil, a sign that it has reached high heat. This should take 45 minutes.

Prepare the turkey by making sure its neck cavity is open at least 2 inches. Place it in a basket neck down. Slowly lower the basket into the oil and cook for 3 to 4 minutes per pound, or until a thermometer inserted in a thigh registers 165°F and the juices run clear. Remove the turkey to rest on paper towels and let sit for 20 minutes before carving.

TURKEY TIPS

If you're starting with a frozen turkey, note that it takes about 24 hours in the refrigerator to thaw a 5-pound bird. So a 12-pound frozen turkey will take 2 days to thaw in the refrigerator.

- If you're pressed for time, you can forgo making the Cajun Turkey Marinade and Cajun Seasoning rub from scratch, and buy ready-made Cajun or Creole seasonings at your local grocery store; I like the Tony Chachere brand.

- Always fry in the open air, *never* inside your garage or home or on a covered patio.

- Be sure the turkey is as dry as possible and lower the bird in the basket slowly and carefully to prevent the oil from flaring up. And don't forget to dispose of your used oil properly—not down the sink or sewer.

CAJUN TURKEY MARINADE

The secret to a very moist and flavorful holiday turkey is to inject it with insane amounts of butter-based marinade. Let the turkey sit overnight in the fridge after injecting so that the bird can soak in all that buttery goodness. I like Louisiana brand hot sauce, but you can use Tabasco, too.

MAKES 2½ CUPS

1 cup lemon juice

1 cup (2 sticks) butter

¼ cup extra-light olive oil

2 tablespoons onion powder

2 tablespoons garlic powder

2 tablespoons Cajun Seasoning (page 180)

1 teaspoon hot sauce, preferably Louisiana brand

1 teaspoon ground red pepper

In a small saucepan over medium heat, combine the lemon juice, butter, oil, onion powder, garlic powder, Cajun Seasoning, hot sauce, and red pepper. Cook, stirring frequently, until the marinade is entirely liquefied and thoroughly combined. While the marinade is hot, use a syringe to inject it into the turkey.

FINGER-LICKIN' GOOD

For the past decade, I've been frying turkey every year for our Thanksgiving holiday. We've even turned the Friday after Thanksgiving into a get-rid-of-your-leftovers potluck party for friends and neighbors. At a recent Thanksgiving, we fried three turkeys, and each one was picked to the bone by night's end. That's how good a fried bird is! As for the bones, use them to make Poultry Stock (page 172) for soups and Rice Porridge with Chicken (page 35).

PANKO-CRUSTED RACK OF LAMB

✧ **When cooked correctly, lamb is incredibly juicy,** tender, and flavorful. Since it's not cheap, many people are too intimidated to attempt to cook a rack of lamb at home, preferring to pay top dollar at expensive restaurants. But I'm here to tell you lamb is really not that difficult to prepare if you buy top-quality lamb and a good meat thermometer. This dish is my go-to recipe when I'm entertaining on short notice. For a beautiful burst of color, serve the lamb with Smashed Purple Potatoes (page 143) and either Haricots Verts with Pancetta (page 132), Roasted Brussels Sprouts with Caramelized Fish Sauce (page 136), or Roasted Beet Salad (page 133). It is vital to use an oven-safe skillet for this recipe so that after you sear the lamb, you can put it straight into the oven.

SERVES 2 TO 4

½ cup panko (Japanese) bread crumbs

2 tablespoons minced garlic

4½ teaspoons chopped fresh rosemary

2 teaspoons salt

1 teaspoon freshly ground black pepper

4 tablespoons olive oil

1 (8-bone) rack of lamb, trimmed and frenched (see "How to French a Rack of Lamb")

1 tablespoon Dijon mustard

Place a rack in the center of the oven and preheat the oven to 450°F. In a large bowl, combine the panko, garlic, rosemary, 1 teaspoon of the salt, and ½ teaspoon of the pepper. Add 2 tablespoons of the olive oil and toss to coat the bread crumbs.

Season the rack of lamb all over with the remaining 1 teaspoon salt and ½ teaspoon pepper. In a large, heavy, ovenproof skillet over high heat, heat the remaining 2 tablespoons olive oil until hot. Sear the lamb all over, 1 to 2 minutes per side. Leave in the pan and set aside.

Brush the lamb all over with the mustard. Spread the panko crumbs on a dinner plate and roll the rack in them until coated all over. Arrange the rack bone-side down in the skillet. Roast in the oven for 12 to 18 minutes, or until desired level of doneness is reached (see note). Remove the lamb to a cutting board, loosely cover it with foil, and let it rest for 5 to 7 minutes. Carve between the ribs and serve warm.

NOTE: *I swear by a digital thermometer and strongly suggest using one. Remove the lamb from the oven when the thermometer reads 5°F less than the desired internal temperature, since it will continue to cook as it rests. For rare (130°F), remove from the oven at 125°F. For medium-rare (135°F), remove from the oven at 130°F. For medium (145°F), remove from the oven at 140°F. For medium-well (160°F), remove from the oven at 155°F.*

I find that the most efficient thermometer is the digital version in which the needle is connected to the digital device by a wire; this allows you to keep the thermometer inside the rack and read the temperature without opening the oven door to jab at the lamb with a thermometer. Constantly opening the oven door lowers the oven temperature, and your lamb will take longer to roast.

WHAT ARE PANKO BREAD CRUMBS?

Panko, or Japanese-style bread crumbs, are crispier and lighter in both texture and flavor than regular ol' bread crumbs. This is why I like to use panko bread crumbs in many of my recipes. You can find them in the international aisle of the grocery store.

HOW TO FRENCH A RACK OF LAMB

To french a rack of lamb is to remove the meat, fat, and gristle from between the bones, leaving them exposed for a nice presentation. You can generally purchase lamb already frenched or ask your butcher to do so, but in the event that you need to do it yourself, here's how.

1. Stand the rack on its side and, using a boning knife, score the meat where the fleshy eye of the rack meats the fatty part, about an inch or two up from the rib tips. Do the same on the other side.

2. Lay the rack fatty side up. Using the scores as a guideline and with the knife perpendicular to the rib bones, cut through the fat, down to the bone. Run the knife through the cut again, making sure to jab the knife in between the bones through to the other side.

3. Flip the rack over, bone side up. Using the scores as a guideline, cut away the meat and fat between all the bones, being careful not to cut past the scores into the eye of the meat.

4. Pull the loosened meat out from between the bones. Use the knife to cut away any remaining meat and fat from between the bones and a towel to pull out the small stubborn bits.

PORK BELLY "SLIDERS"

✧ **Okay, so this isn't a true slider recipe** per se. It's not steamed and does not consist of a scant beef patty; instead, the pork belly is brined and braised, topped with tangy pickled peppers, and stuffed between sweet Hawaiian rolls.

I made these sliders for a pool party, and they were devoured within minutes. They're perfect for feeding a crowd; build them just before serving, or else you risk soggy sliders. If you prefer to skip indulgent pork belly, use pork shoulder instead.

MAKES 24

FOR THE RUB

2½ pounds pork belly, cut into 3 x 6-inch pieces

2 tablespoons kosher salt

1 tablespoon freshly ground black pepper

1 teaspoon ground ginger

1 teaspoon ground allspice

½ teaspoon ground cinnamon

½ teaspoon ground cloves

FOR THE PORK

Salt and freshly ground black pepper

1 tablespoon plus 2 teaspoons extra-light olive oil

2 carrots, chopped

2 stalks celery, chopped

1 small onion, chopped

1 bay leaf

1 teaspoon dried thyme

2 cans (12 ounces each) beer

1½ quarts Poultry Stock (page 172) or low-sodium chicken broth

24 mini Hawaiian rolls, sliced in half crosswise

Spicy brown mustard

48 slices pickled jalapeño chile peppers

TO MAKE THE RUB: Rinse the pork and pat it dry. In a small bowl, combine the salt, black pepper, ginger, allspice, cinnamon, and cloves. Rub the pork liberally with the prepared rub. Wrap tightly in plastic wrap and refrigerate for at least 48 hours.

TO MAKE THE PORK: Rinse the rub off of the pork and pat it dry with paper towels. Season the pork to taste with the salt and pepper. In a Dutch oven, heat the oil over medium-high heat. Sear the pork on both sides until deep golden. Using tongs, remove the pork and set it aside. Drain all but 2 tablespoons of the fat from the Dutch oven. Add the carrots, celery, and onion and cook, stirring frequently, for 10 minutes or until soft and tender. Add the bay leaf, thyme, and beer and, using a wooden spoon, scrape up any bits that are stuck to the bottom. Reduce the heat and simmer for 15 minutes, or until the liquid is reduced by half. Meanwhile, preheat the oven to 350°F.

Return the pork to the Dutch oven and add just enough Poultry Stock to cover. Bake, covered, for 3 hours or until the pork is fork-tender. Remove and discard the bay leaf.

Meanwhile, toast the Hawaiian roll halves. Spread the mustard on each roll top. Slice the pork into 3 × 1-inch pieces. Assemble the "sliders" by stacking 2 or 3 pieces of pork belly on the bottom half of each roll. Top with 2 slices of pickled jalapeño chile pepper and cover with the top bun.

SHAKING BEEF
Bò Lúc Lắc

✦ *Lúc lắc* is the Vietnamese phrase for the sound of the beef shaking in the hot pan. A restaurant in the neighborhood where I grew up serves this dish with a side of Ketchup Fried Rice (page 48) and it's one of the most popular dishes on the menu. The caramelized sear on the outside of the beef with its tender pink center complements the sweetened tomato-based fried rice.

The secret to making this an extraordinary dish is to use top-quality beef. Typically it is made with sirloin steak, but you can up the ante by using rib eye or even filet mignon (depending on how much you like your dinner guests). If you don't have day-old rice in your fridge, forgo the Ketchup Fried Rice and serve this dish with plain jasmine rice.

SERVES 4

FOR THE MARINADE

2 cloves garlic, crushed

1½ tablespoons sugar

1 tablespoon oyster sauce

1 tablespoon fish sauce

1 tablespoon sesame oil

1 teaspoon soy sauce

2 pounds bone-in sirloin, rib eye, or filet mignon steak, trimmed of fat and cut into 1-inch cubes

FOR THE VINAIGRETTE

2 tablespoons rice vinegar

1½ tablespoons sugar

½ red onion, thinly sliced

FOR THE DIPPING SAUCE

Juice of 1 lemon

Salt and freshly ground black pepper

TO SERVE

Green lettuce leaves, coarsely chopped

1 tomato, sliced ¼ inch thick

TO MAKE THE MARINADE: In a large bowl, combine the garlic, sugar, oyster sauce, fish sauce, sesame oil, and soy sauce and stir to combine. Add the meat and turn to coat. Refrigerate for 1 hour.

TO MAKE THE VINAIGRETTE: Meanwhile, in a small bowl, combine the rice vinegar and sugar and mix well. In a separate bowl, combine the onion and 3 tablespoons of the vinaigrette to quick-pickle the onion.

TO MAKE THE DIPPING SAUCE: In a small ramekin, combine the lemon juice with the salt and pepper.

TO MAKE THE BEEF: Heat a wok over high heat. Add half the onion and enough beef to cover the surface of the wok and cook for 1 minute or until seared. Shake the wok to turn the beef and sear for 1 to 2 additional minutes. Repeat with the remaining onion and beef. Remove from the heat and arrange on a plate. Garnish with the tomato slices and lettuce. Drizzle the remaining vinaigrette over the meat and vegetables. Serve with rice and the dipping sauce.

STIR-FRIED VERMICELLI WITH SEARED SCALLOPS

✧ **Stir-fried noodles** are one of my favorite comfort foods. I like them all: Chinese lo mein, Filipino *pancit*, Soy Sauce Stir-Fried Noodles (page 50). There's something about eating your entire meal out of a single bowl that connotes instant comfort. The seared scallops in this recipe, however, dress up the otherwise humble dish and make it an easy but tasty option for a casual gathering.

In the last *MasterChef* Mystery Box Challenge, we were given free rein to make anything we wanted, something we deemed worthy to be in our cookbook should we win the title of MasterChef. I'd learned the hard way throughout the competition that I only did well when I didn't worry about pleasing the judges and just cooked whatever I'd want to eat myself. And because I had yet to use a wok—something I often cook with at home—in the *MasterChef* kitchen, I decided to make these stir-fried noodles using the familiar cookware.

This dish is simple to execute but complex in flavor, which is why it is a great dish to serve when you want to impress but have little time.

SERVES 4

FOR THE NOODLES

3 tablespoons fish sauce

3 tablespoons soy sauce

2 tablespoons Poultry Stock (page 172) or low-sodium chicken broth

1 tablespoon fresh lime juice

1 tablespoon mirin

1½ teaspoons rice vinegar

4½ teaspoons sugar

8 ounces dried rice vermicelli, soaked in cold water for 30 minutes

2 tablespoons canola oil

3 shallots, finely chopped

1 tablespoon minced garlic

1 tablespoon peeled, finely chopped fresh ginger

1 pound oyster mushrooms, halved if large

2 carrots, julienned

2 scallions, thinly sliced

FOR THE SCALLOPS

16 large sea scallops

Kosher salt

2 tablespoons canola oil

2 tablespoons chile oil

8 sprigs cilantro

TO MAKE THE NOODLES: In a small bowl, whisk the fish sauce, soy sauce, Poultry Stock, lime juice, mirin, vinegar, and sugar until the sugar dissolves. Set aside.

Bring a large pot of salted water to a boil over high heat. Prepare a large bowl of ice water. Drain the soaking water from the vermicelli. Add the vermicelli to the boiling water and cook for just 10 seconds. Quickly drain the noodles, then place them in the ice water to cool completely. Drain well.

Heat a large, heavy wok over medium-high heat. Add the canola oil, then stir in the shallots, garlic, and ginger. Cook for 1 minute, or until fragrant and the shallots begin to soften. Add the mushrooms and carrots and stir-fry for 5 minutes, or until they soften slightly. Stir in the vermicelli and the reserved sauce and stir-fry for 30 seconds to coat. Stir in the scallions.

TO MAKE THE SCALLOPS: Season the scallops to taste with salt. Heat a large, heavy sauté pan over high heat. Add the canola and chile oils and swirl to coat the pan, then add the scallops and cook for 2 minutes per side, or until dark brown.

To serve, divide the vermicelli among 4 wide bowls. Top with the scallops, garnish with the cilantro, and serve immediately.

WHY A WOK?

A wok is a large bowl-shaped vessel originally used in Chinese cooking but now found in almost every cuisine. While it can be used, among other things, to steam, braise, or deep-fry, it is most commonly used to stir-fry. The wok's shape helps to distribute heat evenly and thus cook food evenly. The classic wok has a completely round bottom and requires an open flame in a pit stove, but today's average home kitchen with its flat gas or electric burners makes a flat-bottom stir-fry pan a more viable option. The secret to perfect stir-frying is to use a very hot fire and to constantly move the food around in the pan. Cut all your vegetables so that they're uniform in size to ensure they'll cook evenly. Also, make sure the noodles are dried before throwing them in the wok—wet noodles will turn into a soggy mess when stir-fried. Take care not to overcrowd the wok: Stir-fry in small batches if necessary.

MY LAST MEAL
The Fifth Course

There is no question I'd follow up pizza with fried chicken, the version I chose to make for the semifinals, much to Chef Gordon Ramsay's dismay. He didn't understand the logic of my preparing something so simple for such an important stage in the game. But after my salmon fiasco (see Salmon Poke, page 29), I vowed never again to cook something I wouldn't want to eat myself.

If a platter of fried chicken was placed in front of me, I'd go for the drumstick without hesitation. Growing up, when my mama was too tired to cook an elaborate meal for weeknight dinners, she'd boil up chicken drums with a little bit of fish sauce, pepper, and garlic or ginger. Then she'd take the stock from the chicken legs and steam rice in it with turmeric and a bay leaf. It was the simplest of meals, but I find myself some days craving plain ol' lightly seasoned boiled chicken legs, especially after I've been eating very complex, robust foods for days.

My mama always reserved the legs for me. She thought they were the easiest part of a chicken for a child to hold and eat while also being the tastiest (which is why, to this day, dark meat is what I prefer). In fact, I loved chicken legs so much that on the first day of third grade at my new elementary school, my brand-new best friend drew me to the snack line after we finished our lunch. "How 'bout a Drumstick?" she suggested.

"A drumstick?" Images of succulent chicken legs danced through my head.

"They cost a quarter," she said.

"That's it? Twenty-five cents?" I followed my new best friend to the end of the snack line. When we reached the window, I pushed my quarter across the counter and asked for a drumstick. To my utter disappointment, the lunch lady handed me a nut-encrusted ice cream cone.

"The best part of the Drumstick is the last bite, where all the chocolate is," my now-not-so-best friend told me.

But I didn't care. I am probably the only kid in the history of that school who was disappointed over an ice cream cone.

(For the Sixth Course, see page 145.)

THAI BASIL CLAMS
Nghêu Húng Qu

✧ **Thai basil is an herb native to Southeast Asia** and has a distinct flavor similar to licorice, anise, or cloves. It is a perfect complement to almost any protein, from chicken to tofu to seafood. In the ground beef challenge of *MasterChef* Season 3, I made the top 18 with my rendition of Thai basil beef.

I had my first taste of Thai basil clams in a seafood restaurant in my hometown of Houston. It was the least pretentious dish on the table yet the one I was drawn to the most for its umami—all the ingredients worked well with the fresh clams. It turns out Thai basil clams are not hard to make at home; with only 10 ingredients, this recipe can be ready to eat in less time than it takes to watch your favorite sitcom, yet it comes off looking much more complicated.

You can simply serve these clams with jasmine rice. Or, to elevate the presentation, serve them on a bed of rice noodles tossed with the clam sauce.

SERVES 4 TO 6

2 tablespoons extra-light olive oil

8 cloves garlic, minced

6 red chile peppers, seeded and finely chopped

⅔ cup dry white wine

2 tablespoons fish sauce

2 teaspoons sugar

4 teaspoons oyster sauce

Freshly ground black pepper

6 pounds littleneck clams, shells scrubbed and rinsed

2 cups chopped fresh Thai basil leaves

In a large wok over medium-high heat, heat the oil. Add the garlic and cook, stirring frequently, until fragrant. Add the chile peppers and cook, stirring, for an additional 10 seconds or until fragrant. Add the wine, fish sauce, sugar, oyster sauce, and black pepper and bring to a boil. Add the clams, cover, and cook until most of the clam shells open, 4 to 6 minutes. Add the basil, cover, and cook for 1 minute longer. Discard any unopened clams before serving. Divide the clams with their broth among 4 to 6 deep bowls (with or without the rice or noodles) and serve.

SOME LIKE IT HOT

Adjust the number of red chile peppers used in this recipe according to your desired level of spiciness. Removing the seeds reduces the heat factor, too. Always wear plastic gloves when preparing them.

CAJUN CRAWFISH BOIL

✧ **Don't put away that 40-quart pot** and propane tank after Thanksgiving (see Cajun Fried Turkey, page 108)—just 6 weeks later, crawfish season officially begins. (Yes, those Cajuns sure do utilize the giant-pot-o'-food-cooked-outdoors method quite a bit.)

In Cajun country, crawfish boils are a favorite pastime. First, friends and family gather around picnic tables covered with newspapers and trash bags. Then comes the beer for the adults, lemonade or sweet tea for the kids. There is a buzz of excitement as everyone waits for the first round of crawfish to come out of the boiling pot. When it's deemed spicy enough, a steaming-hot 40-quart batch of crawfish and fixin's is poured down the center of the table. People help themselves to the feast, oohing and ahhing as the piles of shells grow. Yes, it's messy, but that's the point: gettin' down and dirty with your neighbors.

SERVES 10

30–40 pounds live crawfish, preferably medium

½ pound (1⅛ cups) salt

2½ pounds Louisiana seasoning powder

3 lemons, halved

4½ teaspoons minced garlic

2½ tablespoons Louisiana hot sauce

2 tablespoons plus 2 teaspoons ground red pepper

1 can (12 ounces) pineapple slices, plus juice

10 medium red potatoes

6 medium onions, halved

9 unpeeled heads garlic

16 small ears corn, halved

1½ pounds sausage links

8 ounces button mushrooms

One hour before cooking, dump the crawfish into a large plastic bin, fill it with water, dump out the water, and repeat. Fill the bin with water a third time, add the salt, and stir.

Fill the basket of a 40-quart pot with crawfish and place the basket in the pot. Fill the pot with enough water to cover the crawfish. Remove the basket and dump the crawfish back into the bin. Check the water level in the pot, dump the water, and refill to that level.

Bring the water to a rolling boil over a propane burner. Add the Louisiana powder, lemons (juice squeezed plus rinds), minced garlic, hot sauce, ground red pepper, and pineapple slices plus juice.

Meanwhile, rinse the crawfish in the bin 2 more times. Working in 2 batches, dump the crawfish, potatoes, onions, corn, and garlic heads into the basket and hose them down under running water.

Slowly lower the basket into the pot of boiling water. Return to a rolling boil and cook for 4 minutes. Turn off the fire, add half the corn, sausages, and mushrooms, and let stand for 20 minutes or until the corn is cooked through. The longer they soak, the spicier the crawfish. Dump the contents of the basket on a newspaper-covered table and enjoy. Cook a second batch and serve accordingly.

MAXIMIZE YOUR CRAWFISH EXPERIENCE

These critters are also known as crayfish, mudbugs, and crawdads, but here in the South, we call them crawfish. They are native to the swamps of Louisiana but have become more widespread as Cajun food has risen in popularity all over the nation. The first step involving the thorough rinsing and salting of the crawfish is called purging, an essential step in properly cooking crawfish that cannot be skipped. Purging draws out all the mud and gunk from the crawfish; skipping this step would result in crawfish that tasted like dirt.

After pulling out a batch of crawfish, discard any with a straight tail—this indicates the crawfish was dead prior to entering the boiling water and thus should not be eaten.

I like to eat my crawfish sans condiments, but here are some options for those who like to dip or add more seasonings:

- Sriracha sauce mixed with mayo
- Cajun Seasoning (page 180)
- Lemon juice, salt, and freshly ground black pepper

Cooked too much crawfish? No problem. Peel the leftovers, freeze the tails, and use them to make étouffée.

HOW TO EAT CRAWFISH: A STEP-BY-STEP GUIDE FOR THE NOVICE

1. With one hand gripping the head of the crawfish, use the other hand to tear the tail from the body.
2. Suck the head (optional)—this is where all the spices are, so beware.
3. Peel back the first two sections of the tail shell farthest from the tail end to expose a little of the tail meat.
4. Pinch the tail end while loosening the meat from the shell with the other hand.
5. Pull the tail meat out from the tail shell.
6. Dip (if you like) and then eat.

WHERE CAN I GET LIVE CRAWFISH?

Because crawfish season runs from January to May, you will find the juiciest crawfish for the lowest prices during these months. I'm lucky to be in the South, where I can go to the nearest grocery store or fish market and purchase them by the bushel. If you live where crawfish are not so readily available, you can order them online and have them shipped to your door.

Chapter 6

On the Side

Side dishes are meant to add variety to a meal and complement the main course. But sometimes, when I'm in the mood for something simple, I'll skip the center of the plate and go straight for the sides. My favorite part of Thanksgiving dinner, for example, is the spread of dishes that surround the turkey—the vegetables, potatoes, greens, and grains. And when it comes to leftovers, I'm inclined to make a second meal of the mashed potatoes, stuffing, Brussels sprouts, and cranberry sauce— no turkey necessary.

It stands to reason, then, that my personal criterion for a worthy side dish is whether it can stand on its own without the benefit of a main course to prop it up. In fact, the perfect side dish is one that makes a good snack, a tasty lunch, or, in some cases, a dinner. On any given day, it isn't unusual to find me grazing on the dishes in this chapter: roasted Brussels sprouts, corn on the cob, hot french fries, or Dirty Rice. Of course, when I entertain at home, I opt for slightly more elegant accompaniments, especially if I'm serving a nice, juicy steak or a handsome rack of lamb (think Haricot Verts with Pancetta or Smashed Purple Potatoes [see photo pages 112–113]). But when lunch or dinner is a casual affair of fried chicken or meat loaf, there's nothing like a mound of mashed potatoes or creamy Broccoli-Rice Casserole to bring on the comfort. You'll notice that potatoes are a personal favorite, as I've included them here prepared three different ways. Whether roasted, fried, or mashed, they never fail to soothe and satisfy. It's a tall order for such a humble vegetable, but then again, the dishes that best sustain us are usually the simplest.

PROSCIUTTO-WRAPPED ASPARAGUS SPEARS

✧ **Salty prosciutto wrapped around crunchy asparagus** spears makes for a quick and easy dish for entertaining; this is my go-to recipe when I want something delectable yet simple. Serve them by themselves as an hors d'oeuvre or as a side dish with Panko-Crusted Rack of Lamb (page 110), Meat Loaf (page 94), or Baked Ziti (page 87). The best part? They can be prepared in less than 30 minutes.

SERVES 4 TO 6

12–24 thin asparagus spears, trimmed

1 tablespoon olive oil

⅛ teaspoon freshly ground black pepper

6 strips prosciutto, halved lengthwise

Preheat the oven to 425°F. Arrange the asparagus spears on a baking sheet. Drizzle the olive oil over them and turn to coat. Season with the pepper. Wrap a single asparagus spear lengthwise with a strip of prosciutto or, if the spears are very thin, bundle 2 together and wrap. Roast until the asparagus is tender when pierced with a fork and the prosciutto is crisp, 10 to 12 minutes. Transfer to a platter and serve warm.

GO FOR THE GRILL

If you happen to be firing up the grill for dinner, put these over the open fire, too. Grill them over medium-low heat, turning them occasionally, until the prosciutto is crisp, 8 to 10 minutes.

HARICOTS VERTS WITH PANCETTA

✧ I rely on this dish when I need an elegant, simple side for a good steak or for Panko-Crusted Rack of Lamb (page 110). Sometimes when I'm cooking up a more casual comfort meal such as Buttermilk Fried Chicken (page 90), Meat Loaf (page 94), or Cajun Fried Turkey (page 108), I like to change up the ingredients to match the Southern feel: regular green beans instead of the French-style haricots verts, red onion instead of shallots, and good old-fashioned bacon instead of pancetta (or I leave it out altogether for a vegetarian option). Butter, garlic, and stock, of course, remain the yummy common denominators.

SERVES 4 TO 6

2 tablespoons butter

2 shallots, chopped

2 cloves garlic, minced

3 strips pancetta, cut into 1-inch pieces

1 pound fresh French-style green beans (haricots verts), ends trimmed

¼ cup Poultry Stock (page 172)

Salt and freshly ground black pepper

In a medium saucepan over medium heat, melt the butter. Cook the shallots, garlic, and pancetta for 5 minutes, stirring frequently, or until the shallots are tender and the pancetta is crisp. Add the green beans and stock. Season to taste with the salt and pepper. Reduce the heat to medium-low, cover, and cook, stirring occasionally, for 15 minutes or until just tender.

ROASTED BEET SALAD

✧ For the switcheroo portion of *MasterChef* Season 3, I ended up with Becky's box, which, among other things, contained beets and goat cheese. I figured I'd roast the beets to unleash their earthy sweetness and pair them with the tart and creamy goat cheese. What came to be was a roasted beet salad that made for a nice, colorful presentation. It's perfect as a first course served before any elegant entrée such as steak, pan-seared fish, or Panko-Crusted Rack of Lamb (page 110).

SERVES 4

6 medium beets with fresh green leaves

1 tablespoon plus ¼ cup olive oil

Kosher salt and freshly ground black pepper

3 tablespoons cabernet sauvignon
or other dry red wine

3 tablespoons white balsamic vinegar

3 tablespoons finely diced shallots

1 teaspoon minced garlic

2 ounces soft fresh goat cheese, crumbled

Preheat the oven to 400°F. Line a heavy baking sheet with foil.

Trim the green leaves from the beets. Wash the 12 smallest leaves and reserve them by wrapping them in a paper towel and storing them in the refrigerator. Scrub the beets and place them on the baking sheet. Drizzle 1 tablespoon of the oil over them and turn to coat. Season to taste with the salt and pepper. Wrap the beets in a foil packet and roast them, turning the packet over occasionally to ensure that they cook evenly, for 45 minutes or until you can poke a skewer through the beets with little resistance. Set aside to cool.

When the beets are cool enough to handle, peel and cut them into ¼ inch-thick rounds. Place in a bowl, cover, and refrigerate until chilled through.

In a medium bowl, whisk together the cabernet sauvignon, vinegar, shallots, and garlic. Whisk in the remaining ¼ cup oil. Season to taste with salt and pepper.

To serve, divide the beet leaves among 4 plates. Pour just enough vinaigrette over the chilled beets to coat. Season to taste. Divide the beets among the plates. Spoon additional vinaigrette over, followed by the goat cheese, and serve.

ROASTED BRUSSELS SPROUTS WITH CARAMELIZED FISH SAUCE

✧ **These are not your grandma's Brussels sprouts!** If you've long associated this vegetable with the bland, gray, soggy dish of your youth, these little nuggets will change your mind. My mind was changed a few years ago when I ordered them at a little gastropub in Austin. Since then, I've noticed they've become all the rage and are popping up on hipster menus everywhere. The secret to this recipe is the caramelized fish sauce that coats each sprout with mouthwatering umami. One taste of these and all memory of bad Brussels sprouts past will be erased.

SERVES 6

FOR THE CARAMELIZED FISH SAUCE

1 tablespoon butter

1 shallot, coarsely chopped

2 cloves garlic, crushed

1 teaspoon peeled and minced fresh ginger

⅓ cup fish sauce

½ cup sugar

2 tablespoons water

Juice of 1 lime

1 stalk lemongrass, white part only, bruised

3 red chile peppers, seeded and finely chopped (wear plastic gloves when handling)

FOR THE BRUSSELS SPROUTS

2 pounds Brussels sprouts, rinsed and halved or quartered, depending on size

2 tablespoons olive oil

3 tablespoons butter, melted

Salt and freshly ground black pepper

1 tablespoon chopped cilantro

1 teaspoon chopped Thai basil leaves

1 teaspoon chopped mint leaves

TO MAKE THE CARAMELIZED FISH SAUCE: In a small saucepan over medium-high heat, melt the 1 tablespoon butter. Add the shallot and cook, stirring frequently, until tender. Add the garlic and ginger and cook, stirring frequently, until fragrant. Transfer to a food processor and puree until smooth. Return the mixture to the saucepan.

Add the fish sauce, sugar, water, lime juice, lemongrass, and chile peppers. Return to medium heat and reduce until the liquid is the consistency of maple syrup.

TO MAKE THE BRUSSELS SPROUTS: Meanwhile, preheat the oven to 425°F. In a medium bowl, combine the Brussels sprouts, oil, and 3 tablespoons melted butter and toss to coat. Season to taste with the salt and pepper. On a baking sheet, arrange the sprouts, cut side down, in a single layer. Roast until the tops of the sprouts are crispy, 20 to 30 minutes. Transfer the sprouts to a serving bowl. Pour the fish sauce over the sprouts and toss to coat. Add the cilantro, Thai basil, and mint and toss again. Serve warm.

SIZE MATTERS

When roasting any vegetable, a uniform cut is essential for even cooking. Brussels sprouts vary greatly in size, so halve or quarter the larger ones to make them all the same size.

GO WESTERN

If you're not in the mood for my Southeast Asian version of Brussels sprouts, simply skip the sauce, roast the sprouts, and toss them with Candied Bacon (page 19) or drizzle them with Balsamic Vinaigrette with Roasted Garlic and Shallots (page 177).

COWBOY CORN ON THE COB

✧ **Corn is one of my favorite things** to eat. Period. There is something incredibly nostalgic about it, especially when it's eaten straight off the grill, preferably poolside with friends. I started making very plain grilled corn on summer breaks during college. I seasoned it only with slabs of butter and a sprinkle of salt and pepper. Sometimes, I scattered a little scallion over the ears. I've come a long way, cornwise, since then. During the Cowboy Challenge of *MasterChef* Season 3, I worked with the ingredients made available to me to make one of my favorite versions. For that recipe, I used sour cream instead of the cream cheese used here and red onion instead of scallions. Either way, it's delicious.

SERVES 6

6 ears corn, preferably sweet

4 tablespoons (½ stick) butter

1 ounce cream cheese

½ teaspoon paprika

½ teaspoon chili powder

¼ teaspoon ground red pepper

Salt and freshly ground black pepper

2 scallions, green parts only, finely chopped

1 lime, cut into 6 wedges

Peel the cornhusks back, remove the silk, and replace the husks over the cobs. In a large bowl of cold water, soak the corn for at least 30 minutes. Meanwhile, heat a grill to medium-high heat.

Place the ears of corn, husks and all, directly on the grill grate, cover, and grill for 15 to 30 minutes, turning once or twice using tongs.

Meanwhile, in a small saucepan, combine the butter, cream cheese, paprika, chili powder, and red pepper. Heat over medium-high heat until the butter and cream cheese melt, stirring occasionally to incorporate the ingredients. Season to taste with the salt and black pepper. Pour into a shallow baking dish.

Shuck the corn and cut them in half, if desired. Place the corn in the butter bath and turn to coat evenly. Transfer to a platter, garnish with the scallions, and serve with the lime wedges.

THE OVEN OPTION

Cowboy Corn on the Cob can be roasted in the oven if a grill isn't available. Preheat the oven to 400°F and, after desilking and soaking the corn, roast it for 15 to 30 minutes directly on the oven rack. Proceed with the rest of the recipe as directed.

QUICK PICKLED CUCUMBERS AND CARROTS
Dưa Chua Ăn Liền Dưa Leo Và Cà Rốt

✧ **I prepared this for Gordon Ramsay,** Graham Elliot, and Joe Bastianich when I auditioned as one of the top 100 contestants for *MasterChef* Season 3. Pickled veggies always pair well with rich proteins because the tart acidity of the pickling juice cuts through the fattiness of the meat. The trick is to slice the cucumbers and carrots thinly so that they absorb the pickling juice quickly.

For my audition, I made this recipe to accompany Clay Pot Catfish (page 72), and it helped me earn a white apron and a spot in the *MasterChef* kitchen. It's also nice with Braised Pork Belly with Egg (page 65), Sticky Rice with Honey-Glazed Chicken and Chinese Sausage (page 61), Braised Pork Riblets (page 66), Grilled Beef Short Ribs (page 71), or Shaking Beef (page 117).

SERVES 6

½ cup rice vinegar

6 tablespoons sugar

2 tablespoons kosher salt

2 small carrots, thinly sliced

2 small cucumbers, thinly sliced

In a large bowl, combine the rice vinegar, sugar, and salt. Stir until the sugar and salt dissolve.

Add the cucumbers and carrots, turning to coat evenly. Cover and refrigerate until desired taste is achieved, about 30 to 45 minutes.

GO PICKLE CRAZY

Try pickling any fruits or veggies using this same method: beets, rutabaga, watermelon, shallots, cabbage, radishes—the list is endless. Just be sure to slice the produce for the best absorption of pickling juice: The denser the vegetable, the thinner you'll want to cut it. For example, beets are denser than watermelon, so you'll want to slice beets thinly while cutting the watermelon into, say, 1-inch cubes.

GARLIC MASHED POTATOES

✧ **Thanksgiving is my absolute favorite holiday:** no stress about shopping for gifts, just good old-fashioned getting together, watching football, and, of course, eating. Mashed potatoes are the ultimate all-American comfort food and a staple for Thanksgiving feasts. Since I serve gravy with Cajun Fried Turkey (page 108), I like to keep the mashed potatoes simple for Thanksgiving—hence this recipe. Otherwise I'll add various herbs and spices, like basil, oregano, parsley, onion powder, and/or paprika, to dress them up when I serve them with Buttermilk Fried Chicken (page 90) or Meat Loaf (page 94).

You can peel the potatoes if you don't like skin, but I prefer to keep it on—not only does it save time, but the skin contains nutrients and offers interesting texture.

SERVES 6 TO 8

1 teaspoon salt

2 pounds russet potatoes, unpeeled, cut into large dice

½ cup (1 stick) butter, cut into 6 pieces, at room temperature

4 ounces cream cheese, at room temperature

1 clove garlic, crushed, or more to taste

¼ cup half-and-half

2 teaspoons minced chives (optional)

Salt and freshly ground black pepper

Bring a large stockpot filled with water and the 1 teaspoon salt to a boil. Add the potatoes and cook, covered, until the potatoes are easily pierced with a fork, 15 to 30 minutes.

Drain and return to the pot. Using a potato masher, mash the potatoes over low heat for 3 minutes or until they are slightly lumpy, letting the heat dry the potatoes. Turn off the heat.

Add the butter, cream cheese, and garlic and continue mashing until fully incorporated. Add the half-and-half 1 tablespoon at a time, mashing after each addition, until the desired consistency is reached. Stir in the chives, if using. Taste and adjust the salt and pepper. Let stand for 5 minutes to thicken. Transfer to a serving dish and serve hot.

PERFECT MASHED POTATOES

You don't want to overmash your potatoes or they may become mealy and watery. Mashing the potatoes over low heat helps release the steam, thereby drying out the potatoes so they won't be watery when you add the other ingredients. For Thanksgiving, I make them the day before and refrigerate them in a covered casserole dish in the fridge. A few hours before serving, I remove the potatoes from the fridge to let them warm to room temperature. I add a few pats of butter on top and bake at 350°F for 20 minutes or until the potatoes are thoroughly warmed through. Then, I simply stir with a wooden spoon and serve.

SMASHED PURPLE POTATOES

✧ **The first time I ever tasted purple potatoes,** it was instant love. It was an autumn afternoon in a restaurant in wine country. One of the courses was a Wagyu beef skewer with a side of purple potatoes, and instead of gushing over the prized Wagyu, I could not stop talking about the potatoes. I flagged down our server to ask how they were prepared, and he gave me a brief rundown. As soon as I returned home, I tried to re-create them for myself in my own kitchen, with quite delicious results.

SERVES 4

1 pound small purple potatoes

⅓ cup whole milk

2 tablespoons butter

Juice of ¼ lemon

1 teaspoon salt

½ teaspoon freshly ground black pepper

Bring a medium saucepan filled with salted water to a boil. Add the potatoes and boil for 15 minutes or until tender but not mushy.

Meanwhile, in a small saucepan, bring the milk and butter to a simmer over medium heat. Set aside.

Drain the potatoes and return them to the saucepan. Heat over low heat to dry them out, stirring occasionally.

Preheat the oven to 400°F. Arrange the potatoes in a single layer on a baking dish. Using a fork, lightly smash each potato without breaking it up. Transfer to a large bowl and toss with the lemon juice. Pour the milk mixture over and toss again. Season with the salt and pepper. Return the potatoes to the baking dish, again arranging them in a single layer. Roast until the potatoes are crispy on the outside, 10 to 15 minutes. Serve warm.

SMALL SPUDS

This recipe can be used with fingerling, new red, or any other small potatoes. But what is it about the purple potato that makes it so special?

Originally from Peru, purple potatoes are dry, starchy, and nutty in flavor. Unlike their white-flesh cousins, purple potatoes contain antioxidants that boost the immune system and fight disease.

DOUBLE-FRIED FRIES

✧ **I grew up on fries.** From McDonald's golden shoestrings to the crinkle-cuts in the school cafeteria, they were among my favorite things to eat. They still are, but I skip my childhood haunts
and make them at home the way I love them, thin and crisp (the secret is to fry them twice) and
sprinkled with sea salt. I like to eat them topped with melted Cheddar, grilled pork belly, and
kimchi—Korean-style spicy pickled Napa cabbage.

SERVES 4

2 russet potatoes, unpeeled,
cut into 4 x ½-inch sticks

Peanut oil

Maldon sea salt

In a large bowl, rinse the potatoes under
running water until the water runs clear. Fill a
separate bowl with ice water and submerge the
potatoes in it. Refrigerate for at least 1 hour.
Drain the potatoes and pat them dry with
cloth towels.

Fill a deep pot with 4 inches of the oil and heat
to 325°F. Add the potatoes a handful at a time
and stir gently to prevent clumping. Fry for
8 minutes or until the potatoes are cooked
through. Remove with a slotted spoon and
drain on paper bags for at least 20 minutes.

Just before serving, reheat the oil to 350°F.
Cook the fries again, working in batches, until
they are crisp and golden, 1 to 2 minutes.
Remove with a slotted spoon and set on wire
racks lined with paper towels to drain the
excess oil. Season to taste with the sea salt
and serve warm.

HOT TIP

Be sure to pat the potatoes very, very dry before dropping them in the fryer. Oil and water don't mix,
and dropping wet potatoes into hot oil can cause the oil to splatter out of the fryer.

FRIES, BEYOND KETCHUP

There's nothing like warm, salty fries. But if you like to jazz them up a bit, try one of these: Cajun Seasoning (page 180), truffle oil and freshly grated Parmesan cheese, minced garlic and a little chopped
rosemary, or spicy mustard, aioli, or Sriracha mixed with mayonnaise.

MY LAST MEAL
The Sixth Course

After a feast of fried dishes, I know I'd crave something light and brothy. A noodle soup would taste so-o-o-o good. My favorites are phở and ramen—the authentic Japanese kind with a broth made from pork and chicken bones simmered for hours, not the instant, 10-for-a-dollar packages from the grocery store. If I had to choose between them, I'd have to stick to my roots and pick phở.

Because making phở is a rather elaborate undertaking, my mama would make enough to fill a 10-quart pot whenever she decided to make it. Even though there were just three of us in the house, that huge pot of soup would last for only 2 or 3 days. it was that good. I vividly remember the weekend mornings when I would awaken to the familiar fragrance of phở; it meant that I'd be eating really well that day, and for several days after that. I prefer my phở straight, without garnishes except for a lime wedge, which I squeeze the juice from before taking that first sip. Occasionally, though, I treat myself to a few additions: hanh tran (the white parts of the scallion blanched in hot phở broth) or hành giấm (thin slices of onion with a dash of vinegar). Both of these add a nice harmonious zing when eaten with the meat.

DIRTY RICE

◇ **Growing up, I loved Popeye's fried chicken** more than I did my own mama's home cooking. (That's sad, I know, but to a Vietnamese-American kid, American food seemed so much more exotic!) So my parents would occasionally acquiesce and bring home the Louisianan Cajun-style fried chicken family meals, which included a large side of dirty rice. I savored the little bits of flavorful ground meat mixed in with the grains but didn't learn until much later in life that it was offal that made the dirty rice taste so good.

Now that I've got the guts to work with offal after cooking with it on *MasterChef* Season 3, I can leave the fast-food version at the drive-thru and make my own at home. Serve this on the side with Cajun Fried Turkey (page 108) or at your next Cajun Crawfish Boil (page 124).

SERVES 6

¼ pound chicken gizzards

2 cups rice

2 cups Poultry Stock (page 172) or low-sodium chicken broth

¼ pound chicken livers, trimmed

1 tablespoon extra-light olive oil

2 cloves garlic, minced

½ pound ground pork

½ cup finely chopped onion

¼ cup finely chopped celery

¼ cup finely chopped green bell pepper

¼ teaspoon ground red pepper or additional to taste

Salt and freshly ground black pepper

In a pot of salted water, boil the chicken gizzards until cooked through. Drain and set aside to cool.

Cook the rice according to package directions, replacing the water with the stock. Set aside.

In a food processor, pulse the gizzards until crumb size. Set aside. Pulse the livers in the food processor until almost liquefied.

In a large skillet, heat the oil over medium heat. Add the garlic and cook, stirring frequently, until fragrant. Add the pork, gizzards, and livers and cook until nicely browned.

Add the onion, celery, and bell pepper. Season to taste with the red pepper, salt, and black pepper, and cook for 10 minutes, or until the vegetables are tender. Gently fold in the rice, then taste and adjust the seasonings.

If the rice is still wet, spread it in a baking dish and bake in a 350°F oven for 20 to 30 minutes or until the rice is dried through.

THE TRINITY

The French have their mirepoix, a mixture of onion, carrot, and celery used as the basis for many sauces and stocks. But the Cajuns have their trinity: 2 parts onion to 1 part celery and 1 part green bell pepper. The trinity is used in everything from jambalaya to gumbo to this Dirty Rice.

BROCCOLI-RICE CASSEROLE

✧ **I first made a version** of this casserole when I was 22 and the first-time host of the family's Thanksgiving dinner. Of course, back then, I was still a novice cook, and so my casserole was entirely made up of not-so-fresh ingredients: frozen broccoli bits, instant rice, processed cheese from a jar, and cream of mushroom soup from a can. Despite the subpar ingredients, everyone raved about the broccoli-rice casserole, helping themselves to seconds and thirds, and even asking for the recipe.

Now, more than 10 years later, I don't have the "novice cook" excuse anymore, so here is an updated recipe that features fresh versions of those packaged ingredients. It is great for potlucks and large gatherings and will always be on my holiday table.

SERVES 8

1½ cups rice

1 quart Poultry Stock (page 172) or low-sodium chicken broth

3½ cups coarsely chopped broccoli

6 tablespoons butter

¼ cup minced onion

1 cup sliced button mushrooms

¼ cup all-purpose flour

1½ cups whole milk

1 large egg, beaten

2¼ cups (9 ounces) grated sharp Cheddar cheese

½ cup crème fraîche

Salt and freshly ground black pepper

Cook the rice according to package directions and set aside.

In a medium saucepan, bring the stock to a boil. Reduce the heat to low and add the broccoli. Simmer for 10 minutes or until the broccoli is al dente. Drain and set aside.

In a sauté pan over medium-high heat, melt 2 tablespoons of the butter. Add the onion and mushrooms and cook, stirring frequently, for 5 minutes or until soft and fragrant. Set aside to cool.

Preheat the oven to 350°F. In a separate medium saucepan over medium-low heat, melt the remaining 4 tablespoons butter. Stir in the flour to make a roux, whisking constantly for 5 minutes or until it reaches a thick, uniform consistency. Add the milk and stir until thoroughly incorporated. Slowly whisk in the egg to temper until thoroughly incorporated. Stir in 2 cups of the cheese, ½ cup at a time, allowing it to melt after each addition.

Transfer the mushroom mixture into a 2-quart baking dish. Fold in the crème fraîche. Add the broccoli, cheese sauce, and rice and season to taste with the salt and pepper. Mix well until the ingredients are thoroughly combined. Bake for 30 minutes. Top with the remaining ¼ cup cheese and bake for 15 minutes longer or until the top is browned and bubbly.

Chapter 7

Something Sweet

I often wonder if the tooth fairy's got my sweet tooth, as these days I'm a fair-weather sweets lover at best. As a child, I ate butterscotch candies straight from the grocery store bin and could plow through a box of chocolate caramels in a single sitting. Now that I'm older, my palate is generally pulled to the bitter end of the spectrum: arugula, extra-dark chocolate, and Indian pale ales. Of course, a yen for the sweet stuff does flare up on occasion, and when that happens, I inevitably turn to classic treats—cookies, pie, and ice cream. When none of those are within reach, I'll satisfy my hankering with a few squares of dark chocolate.

Dessert figures into my repertoire most often when I'm entertaining. I'm not a fancy dessert gal by any stretch—unless you consider a super-fudgy brownie, a bowl of Browned Butter Ice Cream, or my infamous apple pie from *MasterChef* Season 3 as fancy. I do, however, tend to lend an exoticism to my frozen sweets—Kaffir lime and lavender are showcased in my ice creams—but when it comes down to it, I never stray too far from what makes a great ending to a meal. Whether it's creamy, crispy, gooey, flaky, or chunky, these are the textures that comfort every time. I've also included two beloved drinks here: a Peach Sweet Tea that is an homage to my Southern roots and Chicory Iced Coffee the way my dad makes it, thick with sweetened condensed milk. Making it brings back vivid memories of him preparing himself a cup each morning. What could be sweeter than that?

OATMEAL CHOCOLATE CHIP COOKIES

✧ **Chocolate chip cookies** are the ultimate sweet comfort. Chocolate chip *pecan* cookies are the ultimate *Southern* sweet comfort.

My next-door neighbor bakes the most divine chocolate chip pecan cookies I've ever tasted. Despite incessant begging, he will not part with the recipe, which has been in his family for generations. Rather than wait for him to bake me a batch, I came up with my own version, which features chunks of semisweet chocolate, pecans, and oats for a bit of earthy flavor and added texture. If you're the type who believes bacon belongs in desserts, candy a slice or two per my Candied Bacon recipe (page 19), crumble it up, and add it along with the oats. These are especially good warm, but I don't know anyone who would turn away from them at any temperature!

MAKES 30

1¼ cups all-purpose flour

1 cup quick-cooking oats

½ teaspoon baking soda

Pinch of salt

¾ cup packed brown sugar

½ cup granulated sugar

1 cup (2 sticks) unsalted butter, softened

1 large egg

1 teaspoon pure vanilla extract

1 cup (or 6 ounces) semisweet chocolate chips

½ cup coarsely chopped pecans

Preheat the oven to 350°F. In a medium bowl, combine the flour, oats, baking soda, and salt and set aside.

In the bowl of a stand mixer fitted with the paddle attachment, combine the sugars and butter and mix on medium speed until creamy. Add the egg and vanilla and mix until thoroughly incorporated. Turn the mixer to medium-low and add the flour mixture ¼ cup at a time, thoroughly mixing after each addition. Add the chocolate chips and pecans and mix until just combined.

Spoon the batter by the heaping tablespoonful onto ungreased baking sheets, spacing them 2 inches apart. Bake for 15 to 18 minutes or until the edges are golden brown. Transfer the cookies to wire racks to cool.

GINGER-COCONUT TUILES

✧ **I made this tuile** (the French word for *tile*, which is exactly what they look like) in the finale of *MasterChef* Season 3 and used it to complement my Coconut-Lime Sorbet (page 164). The ginger and cool coconut-lime flavors make for a nice contrast, as do the crispy tuiles and the creamy ice cream.

MAKES 12

4 tablespoons (½ stick) unsalted butter

¼ cup sugar

¼ cup Simple Syrup (below)

1 tablespoon whole milk

⅓ cup unsweetened shredded coconut

3 tablespoons peeled, grated fresh ginger

2 tablespoons all-purpose flour

Preheat the oven to 325°F.

In a small saucepan, combine the butter, sugar, and syrup and cook, stirring, over medium-high heat, until the butter is melted and the ingredients are thoroughly incorporated. Stir in the milk, coconut, ginger, and flour and bring to a low boil. Remove from the heat.

Spoon ½-teaspoon-size balls of the mixture onto a baking sheet, spacing them 3 inches apart. Press down lightly on each ball to flatten it slightly. Bake for 8 to 12 minutes, or until flattened, golden, and crispy.

When still warm, drape each tuile over a rolling pin to form a crescent, or leave them flat for a more rustic version.

SIMPLE SYRUP

This syrup will keep, covered and refrigerated, up to 3 months.

MAKES 1 CUP

1 cup sugar

½ cup water

In a small saucepan, bring the sugar and water to a simmer, stirring until the sugar dissolves. Continue simmering for 5 minutes longer. Cool completely, then transfer to a glass jar with a tight-fitting lid.

HUMBLE APPLE PIE

✧ **That's what Gordon Ramsay called it.** Before the pressure test on *MasterChef* Season 3, I'd made apple pie only once before. So when the challenge of baking one from scratch was announced, I was sure I'd be going home that day. I'd long felt that baking, with its exact measures, timing, and heat, was too restrictive for my cooking style. But I wasn't willing to give in to my doubts after I'd gotten so far on the show, so I gave it my all.

From its buttery crust to its fragrant filling, the pie was praised by Chef Ramsay. And thus began my ascent on the ladder of confidence. The keys are not to handle the crust too much and not to be shy with the spices. Serve this with Browned Butter Ice Cream (page 161).

SERVES 8

½ cup (1 stick) unsalted butter

3 tablespoons all-purpose flour

¼ cup water

½ cup granulated sugar plus additional for sprinkling

½ cup packed brown sugar

6 Granny Smith apples, peeled, cored, and sliced

½ teaspoon ground cinnamon

Pinch of ground nutmeg

Pinch of ground cloves

Flaky Pie Crust (page 157)

1 large egg, lightly beaten

In a large saucepan over medium heat, melt the butter. When it foams, add the flour and whisk until dissolved to form a paste. Whisk in the water, the ½ cup granulated sugar, and the brown sugar. Raise the heat and bring to a boil, then immediately reduce to a simmer. Add the apples, cinnamon, nutmeg, and cloves and toss to coat evenly. Cook, stirring occasionally, for 15 minutes or until the apples give slightly when pressed up against the side of the pan.

Preheat the oven to 425°F. On a lightly floured surface, use a lightly floured rolling pin to roll out 1 piece of Flaky Pie Crust dough into a 13-inch round (keep the remaining dough chilled). Fit it into a 9-inch pie plate. Trim the edge, leaving a ½-inch overhang, and chill while rolling out the remaining dough.

Transfer the apple mixture to the pie plate, mounding the apples in the center. Drape the top pie crust over and pinch the edges to seal. Using a sharp knife, cut four 2-inch slits into the crust to allow the steam to escape. Brush the crust with the beaten egg and sprinkle with additional granulated sugar. Bake for 15 minutes, then reduce the heat to 350°F and bake for another 35 to 45 minutes or until the apples are tender and the crust is golden.

FLAKY PIE CRUST

MAKES TWO 9-INCH OR 10-INCH CRUSTS

2 cups all-purpose flour

1 tablespoon sugar

1 teaspoon salt

1 cup (2 sticks) cold unsalted butter, cut into 16 pieces

⅓ cup ice cold water

In the bowl of a food processor, combine the flour, sugar, and salt and pulse several times to blend. Add the butter and pulse until the mixture becomes pea sized. Gradually add the water by the tablespoonful until the dough just comes together. Transfer the dough to a clean work surface and divide it into 2 equal portions. With the heel of your palm, flatten out each dough portion into a 1-inch-thick disk. Wrap each disk in plastic wrap and refrigerate for at least 1 hour before using. Or double wrap each disk in plastic, place in a resealable freezer bag, and freeze for up to 1 month.

DARK CHOCOLATE FUDGE BROWNIES

✧ **I absolutely love dark chocolate** and have since I was little. I was the kid who, at every Halloween, traded all her milk chocolate miniature bars for the Special Dark ones most children find inedible. Call my elfin palate sophisticated—I much preferred the rich bitterness of dark chocolate to milk chocolate, which I found unbearably sweet.

So it stands to reason that I love these brownies—especially with a tall, cold glass of milk, eaten late at night at the kitchen table. I love my brownies fudgy, so moist that they stick to the roof of my mouth before melting on my tongue. That's what these brownies do. I usually make them straight up, but you can add ½ cup of chopped pecans or walnuts for a bit of crunch. Serve them with a scoop of Browned Butter Ice Cream (page 161) or Honey Lavender Ice Cream (page 163) for a real treat.

MAKES 12

1 cup (2 sticks) unsalted butter, softened

4 ounces unsweetened chocolate

2 cups sugar

4 large eggs

1 teaspoon pure vanilla extract

1 cup all-purpose flour

½ cup unsweetened cocoa powder

1 teaspoon baking powder

½ teaspoon salt

Preheat the oven to 350°F. Lightly coat a 13 x 9-inch baking pan with cooking spray.

In a medium saucepan over low heat, melt the butter and chocolate, stirring constantly. Remove from the heat and stir in the sugar. Add the eggs one at a time, mixing well after each addition. Stir in the vanilla.

In a medium bowl, combine the flour, cocoa, baking powder, and salt. Add the dry mixture to the wet ½ cup at a time and mix with a wooden spoon until just combined before the next addition. (Do not overmix—small lumps are okay.) Transfer the batter to the baking pan and bake for 30 minutes, or until a toothpick inserted in the center comes out clean. Cool on a wire rack, then cut into 12 equal pieces.

BROWNED BUTTER ICE CREAM

✧ **Recent food trends are all about the unexpected:** taking different ethnic cuisines and marrying them together in a single dish; transforming the nature of an ingredient so that it resembles something totally different; or, in this case, using a traditionally savory ingredient—browned butter—in a sweet. It gives this creamy dessert a wonderfully nutty flavor. Serve it with a slice of Humble Apple Pie (page 156) for an entirely homemade scrumptious dessert.

MAKES 1 QUART

1 cup whole milk

2 cups heavy cream

1 vanilla bean, split

3 tablespoons salted butter

¾ cup packed brown sugar

5 egg yolks

2 teaspoons dark rum or whiskey

¼ teaspoon pure vanilla extract

¼ teaspoon ground cinnamon (optional)

In a medium saucepan, combine the milk and cream. Using a paring knife, scrape the seeds of the vanilla bean into the milk mixture, then add the pod. Heat the milk mixture over medium-low heat until simmering. Do not bring to a boil. Remove from the heat, cover, and set aside for 1 hour to allow the vanilla to infuse into the liquid.

In another medium saucepan over medium heat, melt the butter. Stir in the brown sugar until it is completely dissolved. Set aside.

Add the milk mixture to the browned butter mixture and stir to thoroughly combine. Return the mixture to medium heat until it reaches 140°F on a kitchen thermometer.

Meanwhile, in the bowl of a stand mixer fitted with the whisk attachment, beat the egg yolks on medium speed for 2 minutes or until they turn pale yellow. With the mixer running, gradually add one-third of the milk mixture to the egg yolks. Add the remaining milk mixture to the bowl and whisk until blended.

Return the mixture to the saucepan and heat over medium-low heat, stirring constantly and scraping the bottom of the pan with a heatproof rubber spatula, until the mixture reaches 170°F and becomes a custard. Pour the custard into a large bowl. Stir in the rum or whiskey, vanilla extract, and cinnamon, if desired. Bring to room temperature by setting the bowl in an ice bath: Fill a larger bowl with ice water and set the bowl of custard in it. Then chill in the refrigerator until the custard reaches 40°F on a kitchen thermometer. Remove the vanilla bean and transfer the custard to an ice cream maker. Proceed according to the manufacturer's instructions.

HONEY LAVENDER ICE CREAM

✧ **I first tasted honey lavender ice cream** at a tiny shop in San Francisco, and I've never forgotten it. It's a combination that defies description—sweet and floral, yes, but that doesn't do it justice. It's a flavor combination you have to experience to appreciate. Of course, I returned home from the trip intent on re-creating what I'd tasted, and after a few trials (and errors!), I came up with my own version, which has become a signature dessert.

MAKES 1 QUART

½ cup honey

4 tablespoons dried lavender flowers

1 cup whole milk

2 cups heavy cream

4 egg yolks

Pinch of salt

¼ cup sugar

In a small saucepan over low to medium-low heat, combine the honey and 2 tablespoons of the lavender flowers. When the honey is warmed through, remove from the heat and let the flowers steep in the honey for 45 minutes.

Place a mesh sieve in a medium bowl. In a medium saucepan, combine the milk, cream, and honey lavender mixture. Heat over medium-low heat but do not bring to a boil. When the milk mixture has reached 140°F on a kitchen thermometer, remove it from the heat and pass it through the sieve, pressing down on the lavender to extract its flavor. Discard the lavender and set aside the mixture.

Meanwhile, in the bowl of a stand mixer fitted with a whisk attachment, beat the egg yolks on medium speed for 2 minutes, or until they turn pale yellow. Add the salt. With the mixer running, gradually add the sugar, whisking thoroughly for 2 minutes longer. With the mixer on medium-low speed, gradually add

one-third of the milk mixture to the egg mixture. Pour the remaining milk mixture into the bowl and whisk until thoroughly incorporated and the mixture resembles custard.

Transfer the custard back to the saucepan. Add the remaining 2 tablespoons of the lavender flowers and heat over medium-low heat, stirring frequently and scraping the bottom of the pan with a heatproof rubber spatula, until the custard reaches 170°F on a kitchen thermometer. Pour the custard into a large bowl and bring it to room temperature by setting the bowl in an ice bath: Fill a larger bowl with ice water and set the bowl of custard in it. Chill in the refrigerator until the custard reaches 40°F on a kitchen thermometer.

Pass the custard through the sieve a second time, pressing down on the lavender with a rubber spatula. Discard the lavender. Transfer the mixture to an ice cream maker and proceed according to the manufacturer's instructions.

COCONUT-LIME SORBET

✧ **When I first visited Vietnam** in 1997, one of my favorite things to eat was a street-cart confection of coconut ice cream served in a coconut shell. I'd sit in the little colorful plastic chairs on the side of the road, a makeshift dining area, and gobble up the cool stuff under the blazing Saigon sun. When I was feeling the heat to create a winning dessert course for the *MasterChef* Season 3 finale, I immediately thought of this to help bring the temperature down. There's nothing more refreshing than tropical coconut flavor, except when you add lime to it, as I do here. Serve this with Ginger-Coconut Tuiles (page 154).

MAKES ABOUT 1 QUART

1½ cups water

⅓ cup sugar

Pinch of salt

2 cans (13.5 ounces each) coconut milk

Zest of 2 limes

2 Kaffir lime leaves

1 vanilla bean, split

In a medium saucepan, combine the water with the sugar, salt, coconut milk, lime zest, and lime leaves. Using a paring knife, scrape the seeds of the vanilla bean into the milk mixture, then add the pod. Bring to a boil over high heat. Remove from the heat and let steep for 2 minutes. Discard the vanilla bean and lime leaves. Pour the mixture into a medium bowl and set it in an ice bath: Fill a larger bowl with ice water and set the medium bowl in it. Chill in the refrigerator until it cools to 40°F on a kitchen thermometer.

Transfer the mixture to an ice cream maker and proceed according to the manufacturer's instructions.

A Sweet Course?

These days, a few squares of bittersweet chocolate satisfy my sweet tooth. I find this curious, as I devoured overly sweet goodies as a child; caramel-filled chocolates were a particular favorite. I'm always game for a really good cookie or top-quality ice cream; and I'm sure if I knew I would never eat a dessert again, my sweet tooth would surface. For nostalgia's sake, I'd likely opt for a stack of Oreos and an ice-cold glass of milk. A simple scoop of Blue Bell's homemade vanilla would do nicely, too.

CHICORY ICED COFFEE
✦ Cà Phê Sữa Đá

The aroma of chicory coffee brewing is one of the fondest memories I have of my dad. As a child, I stole whiffs from his mug on the Formica countertop while he sat on a stool reading the paper, occasionally pausing to screw the top screen of his filter tighter over the grounds. He drank Café Du Monde coffee, the mustard-yellow tin cans serving as knickknack storage containers around the house long after they were empty.

Years later, during a college trip to New Orleans, I had my first Café Du Monde iced coffee in the French Quarter. The coffee is strong but sweetened by the condensed milk and diluted and made more palatable by the melting ice.

To this day, I still have the same single-serving metal French drip filter my dad used to make his coffee. Whenever I am feeling especially nostalgic, I retrieve it from the high shelf of my kitchen, dust it off, and brew chicory coffee with it the same way my dad did.

Drink a glass for breakfast with Sunny-Side-Up Eggs with Toast (page 56) or for brunch with My Mama's Chicken Noodle Soup (page 36).

SERVES 1

2 tablespoons sweetened condensed milk

Ice cubes

2 heaping tablespoons coarsely ground chicory coffee

8–12 ounces very hot water

Pour the condensed milk into an 8- to 10-ounce mug. Fill a tall drinking glass with ice cubes.

Unscrew and remove the top screen from a single-serving metal French drip filter. Pour the coffee grounds into the drip filter and screw the top screen back on until it presses tightly down on the coffee grounds. Set the drip filter on top of the mug of condensed milk.

Pour 8 ounces of the hot water into the drip filter, cover with the lid, and wait for 5 minutes or until all the water has dripped through the coffee grounds into the mug. For stronger coffee, uncover and tighten the top screen; for weaker coffee, loosen the top screen. Pour in more water to fill the drip filter again, cover, and let all the water drip into the mug.

Remove the drip filter and stir the coffee and condensed milk together until well blended. Pour into the glass of ice and give it a quick stir.

WHAT IS CHICORY?

Chicory is made from the root of the endive plant native to Europe and used as a substitute during coffee shortages. Along the same lines, condensed milk was used in *cà phê su'a dá* because fresh milk was too expensive or not readily available. Café Du Monde is the classic brand, but you can use any chicory coffee or even any dark roasted coffee.

PEACH SWEET TEA

✧ **For as long as I can remember,** I've loved my iced tea with no lemon and tons of sugar. I'm talking about 10 packets of sugar per glass! I thought I was just eccentric, but I found out later in life that what I *really* was was a true Southern gal and that what I loved was Southern sweet tea.

When it's humid and almost a hundred degrees outside, as with every Texas summer, I like to brew a pitcher of refreshing sweet iced tea and sip a glass of it on the balcony as the sun sets before me. Sweet iced tea is the quintessential Southern summer beverage, and here, it's made even more charming with fresh peach puree. Go ahead and reward yourself: Kick back, hoist your boots onto the wicker table, and enjoy an ice cold Peach Sweet Tea.

MAKES 1 QUART

⅓ cup loose tea leaves or 7 tea bags

1 quart boiling water

2 ripe peaches, peeled, pitted, and diced

⅔ cup sugar

4 cups ice cubes

½ ripe peach, pitted and thinly sliced

Place the tea leaves or bags in a medium saucepan. Add the boiling water. Steep for 8 minutes or as long as desired.

Meanwhile, in a blender, puree the diced peaches and the sugar. Add the peach puree to the hot tea mixture and stir until well blended and the sugar has melted.

Fill a pitcher with the ice and pour in the peach tea. Garnish the pitcher with the peach slices.

SWEET VARIATIONS

If you omit the peaches altogether from this recipe, what you'll have is a sweet tea base ready to spruce up any way you like it. Replace the peaches with a basket of raspberries for Raspberry Sweet Tea. Alternatively, garnish with mint sprigs for Mint Sweet Tea. Or, if you like your Southern tea stiff and Long Island style, add 4 ounces of vodka and 2 ounces of peach schnapps. To make Ginger Peach Sweet Tea, steep a 2-inch piece of peeled and bruised fresh ginger in boiling water along with the tea leaves.

Chapter 8

A Stock,
Sauces,
Vinaigrettes,
and Seasonings

This chapter is my "extras, et cetera" collection. From classic Vietnamese staples like Savory Caramel Sauce and Fish Sauce Vinaigrette to regional must-haves for southern cuisine like Barbecue Sauce and Cajun Seasoning, this section offers a variety of basics upon which to build your own recipes.

The Savory Caramel Sauce is especially good for braising meats and will give any dish a characteristic Vietnamese flavor. Fish Sauce Vinaigrette is something I grew up eating and is central to so many Vietnamese foods: Toss it with a cool salad of vermicelli, grilled meats, and fresh veggies; or use it as a dipping condiment for eggrolls and lettuce wraps. Both of these sauces are essential to Vietnamese cookery yet versatile enough to adapt to Western ingredients whenever you want to update an old recipe.

Then there are the bases for classic American foods like No-Cook Pizza Sauce, Barbecue Dry Rub, and Poultry Stock—all of which you can also use to create dishes with your own personal flair. Forgo the prosciutto and arugula, and add your own toppings to the pizza using the quick and easy No-Cook Pizza Sauce. Use the Barbecue Dry Rub to make brisket or baby back ribs. The Poultry Stock can be used to make chicken noodle soup or as a substitute for water in most recipes for extra unctuousness.

These stock, sauces, and seasonings are simply building blocks for your comfort food creations, so let your imagination run wild when cooking with them. Don't be afraid to experiment; with these few fundamental recipes, the possibilities are endless.

POULTRY STOCK

✧ **My mama taught me never to waste food.** This went for not only what she put on my plate, but the ingredients most people might discard, including chicken and duck bones. A lot of rich, fatty flavor can be extracted from animal bones to make a flavorful stock. And there's nothing like homemade stock when you're making just about any soup, stew, or rice. What's more, it freezes beautifully—and for up to 3 months. I use it in my Rice Porridge with Chicken (page 35) and My Mama's Humble Tomato Soup (page 34), or simply in lieu of water in any savory recipe to give a dish more umami. I especially like to use it to cook rice, then serve the rice with steamed chicken.

The ingredient portions that follow are for chicken or duck stock. If you're using the bones of an entire turkey, add an extra carrot and stalk of celery.

MAKES 4 TO 6 QUARTS

3 pounds chicken necks, trimmed

1 (6–8-pound) bird carcass

2 carrots, cut into chunks

2 stalks celery, cut into chunks

2 medium yellow onions, coarsely chopped

1 bay leaf

1 teaspoon peppercorns

Using a meat cleaver, chop the chicken necks to expose the marrow.

Place the chicken necks and bird carcass in a large stockpot, chopping the carcass to fit, if necessary. Fill the stockpot with cold water to cover the necks and carcass by 1 inch. Add the carrots, celery, onions, bay leaf, and peppercorns. Bring to just below a boil over high heat. Reduce the heat to medium-low and simmer, uncovered, for at least 2 hours and up to 4 hours. Do not let boil. Cover, reduce the heat to medium-low, and simmer for 4 hours longer, occasionally skimming from the surface any foamy scum that has accumulated.

Remove the pot from the heat and let cool. Once cool, strain the stock through a chinois or cheesecloth-lined sieve into a heatproof bowl or pot. Discard the solids. If using immediately, skim the fat from the surface. If not, let cool completely, then transfer to rigid, airtight containers, leaving $1/2$ inch of space between the liquid and the lid, and refrigerate. Remove the layer of hardened fat that accumulates on the surface before using. The stock will keep, refrigerated, for up to 3 days or in the freezer for up to 3 months. Thaw in the refrigerator before using.

ROOM AT THE TOP

More times than I care to count, I have opened my freezer to find the lids bursting off the containers of stock I've patiently prepared. The reason? I filled the containers to the top and didn't allow for the expansion that happens when a liquid freezes. Prevent a freezer explosion by leaving at least $1/2$ inch of space at the top of the container.

SAVORY CARAMEL SAUCE
Nước Màu

◇ **This savory sauce** is liberally used in Vietnamese cooking to lend depth—an almost coffeelike flavor—to all manner of braised and grilled meats and fish. You'll notice I am quite fond of it, as I use the sugar and water combination in various proportions in Clay Pot Catfish (page 72), Braised Pork Belly with Egg (page 65), and Braised Pork Riblets (page 66). The sauce can be stored in an airtight glass jar in a cool, dark place indefinitely. Do not refrigerate.

MAKES 1 CUP

1 cup water

1 cup sugar

Place 1/2 cup of the water in a small saucepan. In a medium skillet, heat the sugar and remaining 1/2 cup water over medium-high heat, stirring frequently, for 3 minutes or until the sugar dissolves. Reduce the heat to low and cook for 15 minutes or until the mixture turns deep, dark brown, the color of molasses. Meanwhile, bring the saucepan of water to a boil.

Just as the sugar begins to smoke, remove the skillet from the heat and gently swirl it to cool. Immediately add the boiling water to prevent the caramel sauce from hardening. Stir briefly to incorporate the ingredients. Let stand to cool to room temperature before using.

SOY-CHILE DIPPING SAUCE

I made this up on the fly as an accompaniment to my Sweetbread Nuggets (page 14) during the offal challenge on *MasterChef* Season 3. It's a very versatile sauce—it covers a wide range of the flavor spectrum from salty to sour to spicy—and is perfect for many East Asian snacks, including dumplings and chicken nuggets.

MAKES ABOUT 1 CUP

½ cup soy sauce

¼ cup apple cider vinegar

2 tablespoons sugar

2 tablespoons peeled, minced fresh ginger

4 jalapeño chile peppers, thinly sliced into rounds (wear plastic gloves when handling)

2 teaspoons fresh lime juice

Salt

In a small bowl, whisk the soy sauce, vinegar, sugar, ginger, jalapeño chile peppers, and lime juice to blend. Season to taste with salt.

BARBECUE SAUCE

This barbecue sauce is perfect for Pulled Pork Sandwiches (page 93) or to serve on the side with a great rack of ribs. The bacon adds fatty richness to the sauce, the mustard and apple cider vinegar keep it tangy, the ketchup and brown sugar preserve the sweetness, and the soy sauce and Sriracha add a little Asian oomph. Leave the bottled barbecue sauce on the store shelf; now you're making your own.

MAKES 3 CUPS

1 strip bacon, cut into 1-inch pieces

2 cloves garlic, crushed

¼ yellow onion, coarsely chopped

1 tablespoon butter

1 cup ketchup

1 cup apple cider vinegar

2 tablespoons spicy brown mustard

2 tablespoons brown sugar

2 tablespoons Sriracha sauce

1 tablespoon soy sauce

1 tablespoon Worcestershire sauce

½ teaspoon ground red pepper

Salt and freshly ground black pepper

In a medium saucepan over medium heat, cook the bacon until crisp. Remove with a slotted spoon, leaving the drippings in the pan. Remove the pan from the heat.

In the bowl of a food processor, puree the bacon, garlic, and onion.

Over medium heat, melt the butter in the same saucepan. Add the onion puree and cook until browned, stirring frequently. Add the ketchup, vinegar, mustard, brown sugar, Sriracha, soy sauce, Worcestershire, and red pepper. Bring to a simmer, reduce the heat to low, and continue to simmer for 8 minutes or until the sauce thickens slightly. Season to taste with the salt and black pepper.

NO-COOK PIZZA SAUCE

✧ **Pizza is one of my favorite foods,** so by default, pizza sauce is too. The perfect pizza sauce should contain just the right blend of herbs and spices, in just the right proportion to the sauce. It should be easily spread onto pizza dough, but not runny. I've come up with a sauce that is supereasy to make and requires no cooking at all. Just blend, let rest, and ladle onto the dough.

MAKES 2 CUPS

1 can (4 ounces) tomato paste

1 cup warm water

¼ cup extra-virgin olive oil

1 clove garlic, minced

½ teaspoon sugar

½ teaspoon onion powder

¼ teaspoon dried oregano

¼ teaspoon dried basil

Salt and freshly ground black pepper

In a small bowl, combine the tomato paste, water, and olive oil and stir to thoroughly incorporate. Add the garlic, sugar, onion powder, oregano, and basil. Season to taste with the salt and pepper and mix well to combine. Let stand for at least 1 hour at room temperature to allow the flavors to meld.

BALSAMIC VINAIGRETTE WITH ROASTED GARLIC AND SHALLOTS

✧ **I love a good balsamic vinaigrette** with any salad, and the best kind of balsamic vinaigrette is the kind you make at home with roasted garlic and shallot. Toss this on the Roasted Brussels Sprouts with Caramelized Fish Sauce (page 136) in place of the fish sauce, on the Roasted Beet Salad (page 133) in place of the vinaigrette, or on any vegetable or salad, for that matter.

MAKES ½ TO ¾ CUP

1 clove garlic, unpeeled

1 small shallot, unpeeled

2 tablespoons extra-light olive oil

⅓ cup balsamic vinegar

¼ cup extra-virgin olive oil

1½ tablespoons brown sugar

1 tablespoon honey

Juice of ½ lemon

Salt and freshly ground black pepper

Preheat the oven to 350°F. In a small bowl, toss the garlic and shallot with the extra-light olive oil. Place on a baking sheet and roast for 5 minutes or until just tender. Let cool, then peel. Mince the garlic and thinly slice the shallot.

In a small bowl, combine the garlic, shallot, vinegar, extra-virgin olive oil, sugar, honey, lemon juice, and salt and pepper to taste. Whisk until the ingredients are blended and the sugar is dissolved. Let stand for at least 30 minutes to allow the flavors to meld. The vinaigrette will keep, refrigerated, for up to 1 week.

FISH SAUCE VINAIGRETTE
Nước Mắm Chấm

→ **I love this vinaigrette so much** I could drink it like juice! It is a staple of Vietnamese cuisine, served in traditional dishes such as egg rolls, bowls of vermicelli, broken or short-grained rice plates, grilled meats, sizzling coconut crepes, and more. Sometimes I like to break tradition and serve it with, say, Brussels sprouts in order to put a Vietnamese spin on a non-Asian dish. This vinaigrette packs a flavorful punch with the sweetness from the sugar, sourness from the lime juice, saltiness from the fish sauce, and heat from the garlic and peppers.

MAKES 2 CUPS

2 cloves garlic, minced, or more to taste

2 red chile peppers, seeded and sliced or minced, or more to taste (wear plastic gloves when handling)

¼ cup lime juice

1 cup water

½ cup fish sauce

¾ cup sugar

In a small bowl, combine the garlic, chile peppers, and lime juice. Set aside.

In a medium bowl, whisk together the water, fish sauce, and sugar until the sugar is completely dissolved. Whisk in the garlic and lime juice mixture and let stand for 30 minutes to allow the flavors to meld.

CAJUN SEASONING

✧ **Add a kick to any of your dishes** with a pinch or rub of this addictive seasoning. I love to sprinkle it on Cowboy Corn on the Cob (page 139) or into Dirty Rice (page 146) and use it as a condiment for the Cajun Crawfish Boil (page 124), but most importantly, rub it all over your bird for a spectacular Cajun Fried Turkey (page 108). I often use this seasoning to flavor chicken, shrimp, or fish for quick weeknight meals. You can double or triple the ingredients to make a larger portion. Just store in an airtight container to use as you would salt and ground black pepper.

MAKES ¾ CUP

2½ tablespoons paprika

2 tablespoons garlic powder

2 tablespoons onion powder

2 tablespoons salt

1 tablespoon ground red pepper

1 tablespoon freshly ground black pepper

In a jar with an airtight lid, combine the paprika, garlic powder, onion powder, salt, red pepper, and black pepper. Shake well until thoroughly combined. Stored in a cool, dark place, the seasoning will keep for 3 months.

BARBECUE DRY RUB

✧ **Being a Texan, I couldn't write** a cookbook without including a barbecue recipe. The quality of a dry rub is the key to great barbecue. It should be so robust that it infuses the meat with its very distinct flavor. This dry rub is versatile enough to be used on pork, chicken, or beef. I especially like to rub it onto a pork shoulder for Pulled Pork Sandwiches (page 95) or on a rack of ribs. The recipe can be doubled directly so that you have some on hand when the inspiration hits.

MAKES 1½ CUPS

½ cup paprika

¼ cup packed brown sugar

2 tablespoons kosher salt

2 tablespoons garlic powder

2 tablespoons onion powder

1 tablespoon freshly ground black pepper

1½ teaspoons ground red pepper

1½ teaspoons dried oregano

1½ teaspoons dried thyme

1 teaspoon ground cumin

1 teaspoon ground mustard

1 teaspoon chili powder

In a jar with a tight-fitting lid, combine the paprika, brown sugar, salt, garlic powder, onion powder, black pepper, red pepper, oregano, thyme, cumin, mustard, and chili powder. Shake until thoroughly combined. The rub can be stored in a cool, dark place for up to 3 months.

Glossary

BAMBOO ROLLING MAT (or MAKISU in Japanese): A thin, flexible mat made of bamboo sticks bound together with cotton string, approximately 9.5 x 9.5 inches, used to make *maki,* or Japanese rolls wrapped in seaweed. Cover with plastic wrap prior to using for easy clean-up. After use, wash with gentle soap and water, and dry thoroughly.

BARBECUE: The term *barbecue* is often a misnomer when used to describe cooking meat, fish, or other foods over an open flame on a grill. This quick-cooking method should really be called "grilling." In the United States, barbecuing involves slow-cooking meats outdoors over the smoke of a wood or charcoal fire. *Barbecue* can also refer to the foods cooked in such a manner, the pit or apparatus in which the foods are cooked, or the meal or gathering at such an event.

BEAN SPROUTS: The sprouts of mung beans used in Asian cuisine. They add a crisp texture (rather than flavor) to a dish and can be eaten raw, blanched, or stir-fried.

BIRD'S-EYE CHILE: Also known as Thai chile, a small, conical, very hot pepper, usually red, orange, or green in color. It measures roughly 50,000 to 100,000 Scoville units.

BLOOD ORANGE: A citrus fruit with crimson flesh that gets its distinct color from pigment developed in regions with low nocturnal temperatures, as in the Mediterranean. The flesh and juice are slightly sweeter than that of the regular orange and contain mild raspberry overtones. Oranges or mandarin oranges can be substituted.

BRAISING: A cooking technique in which the ingredient is first seared and then cooked in a closed vessel in liquid over low heat for a long period of time. It is most often used to prepare tougher cuts of meat, as the method aids in breaking down the connective tissue in the protein, bringing about a tender result. Braising can be done in *clay pots*, Dutch ovens, Crock-Pots or slow cookers, or *pressure cookers*.

CAJUN: Pertaining to the people from the bayou regions of southern Louisiana of French Canadian descent known as the Acadians, or their cuisine, which is characterized by hearty, spicy country dishes often prepared in a single pot. Cajun cuisine is not to be confused with Creole cuisine which springs from those of mixed heritage—Spanish and French aristocrats blended with African or Caribbean blood—and is typically more continental in character. Common Cajun ingredients include rice, corn, okra, seafood and game, garlic, cayenne pepper, and the trinity (onion, celery, and bell pepper). Specialty dishes include boudin sausage, gumbo, and jambalaya.

CHINESE BROCCOLI (or KAI LAN or GAI LAN in Cantonese): A leafy green vegetable with flat, thick leaves and thick stems related to broccoli, it has a flavor similar to that of broccoli but more bitter.

CHINESE SAUSAGE (or LAP CHANG in Cantonese): A dried, hard sausage usually made of pork with a high fat content. It is typically smoked, sweetened, and seasoned with *soy sauce* and rice wine.

CHINOIS: A conical sieve used for straining sauces and soups or puréeing foods. It is especially useful for separating solid matter from soups after flavors have been extracted, resulting in a clearer, purer broth.

CLAY POT: A lidded earthenware vessel that can either be glazed or unglazed. It is best suited for *braising*, stewing, or any method that involves cooking food at low temperatures for long periods of time. Because clay is a porous material, it absorbs liquid and releases it during cooking, resulting in moister meats. Clay pots can be found at Asian specialty markets. Before initial use, fully submerge the pot in water and soak overnight. Then scrub with a brush to remove any clay bits. Glazed clay pots require only this initial soak, but unglazed pots need to be soaked for 15 minutes prior to each use. Asian clay pots can be used both on the stove and in the oven. Always avoid sudden changes in temperature, as this could crack the pot. If using stove-top, start with a low fire and gradually increase it to medium at most, 5 minutes later. If placing in the oven, always begin with a cold, unpreheated oven. Clean the pot once it's cooled, scrubbing with warm water and maybe a little baking soda. Don't use detergents, as the strong chemicals could penetrate the clay and affect the taste of future foods. Never, ever run the clay pot through the dishwasher.

COCONUT: The large seed of a tropical palm tree. On the outside is a hard, brown shell, while inside is clear liquid and white flesh. Coconut milk, which is made by soaking the flesh in warm water and then squeezing it through cheesecloth, is used in many Southeast Asian dishes, such as *curries*. Coconut water is simply the clear juice that is found inside young coconuts. Coconut soda is sweetened, carbonated coconut extract; Coco-Rico brand is the most popular for Vietnamese cooking.

COOKING SAKE: An alcoholic Japanese beverage made from fermented rice, reserved for cooking.

CRAWFISH: Also called crayfish or crawdads depending on the region, crawfish are freshwater crustaceans resembling miniature lobsters. They are primarily found in the southeastern United States, especially Louisiana, where they are consumed particularly in *Cajun* cuisine. The tail meat is the most edible, although sometimes the claw meat can also be eaten, depending on the size of the crawfish.

CURRY: From South Asian cuisine, *curry* originated from the word *kari*, which means "sauce" in Tamil. Today, curry can be found all over the world using a country's local ingredients. The term *curry* is now understood to describe a South Asian–inspired dish consisting of meats, vegetables, and strong spices usually eaten with rice. Curry can also refer to the spice known as curry powder.

DAIKON: Also known as white radish, a large, mild-tasting Asian radish that resembles a large carrot in appearance. It is often *pickled*, used as a garnish, or simmered in a soup or stew.

EGG ROLL SKIN: The sheet used to wrap a meat-and-vegetable filling and subsequently fried to make egg rolls. Vietnamese egg roll skin is different from that used for Chinese egg rolls in that when fried, it produces a thinner, flakier, crispier skin. Egg roll skin is generally made from flour, water, and egg. It can be found in the freezer section of an Asian market. Rice paper can be substituted when making egg rolls; soak briefly in hot water to reconstitute before filling and wrapping.

FISH SAUCE (or NƯỚC MẮM in Vietnamese or NAM PLA in Thai): A salty and strong-smelling condiment mostly used in Southeast Asian cuisine and made from the extracted liquid of fermented anchovies and salt. Fish sauce can be eaten as a condiment like *soy sauce*, used in marinades, or added during the cooking process as seasoning. Look for fish sauce made in Vietnam or Thailand with a short list of ingredients: just fish extract, salt, and water. Quality fish sauce should be a lighter reddish-brown color like tea.

FLATBREAD: Thin, often (but not always) unleavened bread made by rolling out a dough consisting of flour, water, and salt. There are flatbread varieties all over the world, including South Asian naan and chapati, Jewish matzo, Mediterranean pita, Ethiopian injera, and Italian focaccia and pizza.

40-QUART POT WITH BASKET: An oversized stockpot with lid and basket insert used for outdoor cooking to prepare, among other things, Cajun Fried Turkey (page 108) and Cajun Crawfish Boil (page 124). To be used with a *propane burner and tank.*

GALANGAL: Sometimes called blue ginger, a rhizome often used in Asian cooking. It is related to ginger but possesses a stronger taste.

GREEN PAPAYA: The unripened papaya fruit with lightly crisped texture used in Southeast Asian salads, stews, and *curries.*

HARICOTS VERTS: French-style green beans that are longer and thinner than the American variety.

HOISIN SAUCE: A Chinese condiment made of starch, water, sugar, soybeans, white vinegar, salt, garlic, and chile pepper. It can be used to flavor a Vietnamese noodle soup called *phở* or the Chinese dish Peking duck.

JICAMA: Sometimes called Mexican yam or Mexican turnip, the edible root originally from Mexico that first spread to the Philippines during Spanish colonization and subsequently to other Asian countries. Because of its crisp texture, it is often eaten fresh in salads.

KAFFIR LIME: Indigenous to South and Southeast Asia, the citrus fruit's rind can be ground into a paste for *curries* to add an aromatic, astringent flavor. The leaves are commonly used to flavor soups, such as *tom yum* from Thailand or *canh chua tôm* (Sour Prawn Soup, page 44) from Vietnam. The juice of Kaffir limes is usually considered too acidic for consumption.

LEMONGRASS: Native to India and tropical Asia, a fragrant, tropical herb stalk that yields a citrus oil. It is widely used in Southeast Asian cuisine to flavor soups, stews, and *curries.* It is also cooked with meats and seafood. Although the entire stalk can be chopped up into smaller pieces for cooking, it is generally the thicker, yellow bottom third of the lemongrass that is used; the stalk should be bruised or smashed to release the essential oils prior to adding to foods.

MAGGI SAUCE: A vegetable protein–based seasoning sauce originating in Switzerland, with a salty, slightly sweet, tangy, umami flavor.

MANDOLINE: A kitchen tool consisting of a flat frame with adjustable cutting blades used for cutting vegetables with precision. Various cut styles include the slice, batonnet, and julienne.

MIRIN: A sweet Japanese cooking wine made of rice and used to brighten up the flavor of a dish, especially fish.

OFFAL: The entrails or internal organs of an animal used for food. Various types of offal include tongues, *sweetbreads*, hearts, stomachs, kidneys, and livers. Once considered the less desirable parts of an animal, offal has recently moved into more mainstream American cuisine due to the rise in popularity of the nose-to-tail philosophy, in which the animal's entire carcass is used for food, leaving nothing to waste.

OXTAIL: The tail of a bovine used in soups or stews.

OYSTER SAUCE: A condiment made from sugar, salt, water, cornstarch, and oysters. Oyster sauce lends a savory flavor to meats and vegetables (especially *Chinese broccoli*) and is primarily used in Cantonese, Thai, Cambodian, and Vietnamese cuisines.

PALM SUGAR: A sweetener usually made by collecting the sap from the stem of a date palm and boiling until it thickens. Palm sugar is used in South and Southeast Asian cuisines and offers a more robust flavor than typical granulated white sugar.

PANKO: A Japanese flaky bread crumb used to add a crunchy texture to fried foods. It is made by passing an electric current through the bread dough during baking and has a crispier, airier texture than the bread crumbs used in Western cuisine. A classic Japanese dish utilizing panko is *tonkatsu*, a fried pork cutlet served sliced over rice with shredded cabbage and a sweet sauce for dipping.

PICKLING: The act of preserving foods in a brine, vinegar, or similar solution to produce lactic acid during fermentation. The resulting taste is often salty and/or sour.

PIZZA STONE: A flat stone or piece of ceramic used to distribute heat inside the oven evenly to flatbreads, pizzas, or other baked goods. Because the surface is porous, it aids in moisture absorption, which results in a crispier crust. Like *clay pots*, a pizza stone should avoid quick changes in extreme temperature in order to prevent cracks. This means placing the stone in the oven before preheating it, and only removing it post-cooking only once the oven has been turned off and the stone has cooled. Clean the pizza stone with warm water and avoid detergents, as the stone may absorb the chemicals and affect the taste of foods cooked on it later. Never clean the pizza stone in a dishwasher.

PRESSURE COOKER: An airtight vessel in which food can be cooked quickly under steam pressure. Pressure cooking simulates *braising* or simmering for long periods of time and reduces the cook time to about a third of the conventional cook time.

PROPANE BURNER AND TANK: A large burner attached to a propane gas tank that is used outdoors to cook large food items or large quantities of food. To be used in conjunction with a *40-quart pot with basket*.

RICE: The seed of a swamp grass cultivated for food. Rice is a staple of many cuisines, including Asian and African. Jasmine rice, which originated in Thailand and is largely consumed by Southeast Asians, is a fragrant, long-grained rice. Sticky rice, also called glutinous or sweet rice, is a rice that becomes extra sticky once cooked (hence the term *glutinous*). The Japanese and Koreans eat a sticky, short-grained rice. In Japanese cuisine, sushi rice is made by adding rice vinegar, sugar, and salt. Basmati rice is an aromatic, long-grained variety traditionally from Pakistan. The white rice called for in American dishes such as Dirty Rice (page 146) or Broccoli-Rice Casserole (page 147) is a long-grained rice that is less aromatic than jasmine and basmati rice and less sticky than Japanese and Korean rice.

RICE COOKER: An electric apparatus used to steam rice.

SASHIMI: A Japanese dish of bite-sized, thinly sliced raw fish usually eaten with *soy sauce*, *wasabi*, and paper-thin shreds of *daikon*. The term *sushi* refers to any food served with sushi rice (or *sushi-meshi* in Japanese), including *nigiri* (a small oblong ball of sushi-meshi topped with wasabi and a bite-sized raw piece of fish or other seafood) or *maki* (a cylindrical roll containing sushi-meshi, *seaweed*, and other ingredients shaped by a *bamboo rolling mat* and sliced into bite-size pieces).

SCALLION: Also known as green onion, an onion relative, characterized by long, hollow green leaves and a small bulb. It has a milder taste than onion and can be eaten raw or cooked.

SEAWEED (or NORI in Japanese or KIM in Korean): An edible seaweed eaten either fresh or dried in sheets. Nori is typically used to make rolled sushi *(maki)* by utilizing a *bamboo rolling mat.*

SESAME OIL: A vegetable oil derived from sesame seeds, often added to Indian, Chinese, Japanese, and Korean foods for flavor.

SHALLOT: A small bulb resembling an onion, but with a slightly sweeter, milder flavor than the onion. Like garlic, shallots develop cloves that form bulbs. Shallots can be sautéed, pickled, or deep-fried, among other methods.

SHRIMP PASTE: Fermented ground shrimp mixed with salt commonly found in Southeast Asian dishes. Shrimp paste is highly pungent and used to add a briny, umami flavor to soups, stews, sauces, and *curries.*

SOY SAUCE: A seasoning made by fermenting soybeans in salt and water, and used as a condiment or flavoring additive during the cooking process. Light soy sauce, which is lighter in color and thinner in consistency, comes from the initial pressing of the fermented soybeans and is considered premium quality. Light soy sauce is mainly used for seasoning. Dark soy sauce, which comes from later pressings and often contains caramel, is thicker, of lesser quality, and mostly used to add color during cooking. Japanese soy sauce (or *shoyu*) uses an even ratio of soybeans to wheat, resulting in a milder, sweeter flavor than its Chinese counterpart. Soy sauce can be mixed with various ingredients (such as vinegar and peppers) to make a dipping sauce. Like *fish sauce*, soy sauce is already fermented and thus can be stored in a cool, dark place.

SPIRAL TURNER: Also called a turner slicer and originally from Japan, a kitchen tool with a hand crank used to cut vegetables into spiral slices. Useful for preparing vegetables such as cucumber and *daikon* for Green Papaya Salad (page 59).

SRIRACHA SAUCE: Called "rooster sauce" or "cock sauce" in the United States, a spicy condiment originating from Thailand and made of chile peppers, distilled vinegar, garlic, sugar, and salt. Sriracha is frequently served alongside *hoisin sauce* as a condiment to the Vietnamese noodle soup called *phở*.

STAR ANISE: A spice used in South and Southeast Asian cooking with an aroma and flavor similar to licorice. It is an essential ingredient in Chinese five-spice powder, Indian garam masala, and the Vietnamese noodle soup called *phở*.

STIR-FRYING: The act of frying foods rapidly, usually in a *wok*, over high heat while stirring quickly. The term *stir-fry* also refers to the dish cooked in such a way.

SWEETBREADS: Considered *offal*, typically the thymus gland (but sometimes the pancreas) of an animal.

TUILE: A thin wafer or cookie usually made of almonds, named for the French word for *tile*.

WASABI: The thick green root of a Japanese plant that is made into powder or paste, used in Japanese cuisine (especially sushi), and tastes like horseradish.

WOK: A large, round-bottom vessel used in Chinese cookery. As a true wok has an entirely curved bottom, it usually requires a special device to hold it over the open fire. Stir-fry pans are roughly the same shape as a wok but have a flattened bottom for stabilization over a stovetop. The size and shape of the wok aid in quick, even cooking necessary for *stir-frying*. Ingredients should be cut in uniform size to ensure even cooking. In addition to stir-frying, woks can also be used to, among other methods, steam, deep-fry, pan-fry, or *braise* foods.

YUZU: A citrus fruit originating from east Asia and tasting of sour mandarin orange and grapefruit. Unlike other citrus fruits, the yuzu has the ability to withstand hardy frost. Yuzu zest is often used to garnish dishes while the juice is used to season much like a lime. The actual yuzu fruit may still be difficult to find in the United States; in this case, bottled yuzu juice, paste, or powder or lime or lemon juice can be substituted.

Acknowledgments

This project would not have been possible without the support of many. I would like to express my sincerest gratitude to those who have played an instrumental role in the creation of this cookbook. A very big thank-you to Rodale and Shine America for making it happen, especially the editors and artists who took my cluttered notions and carried them to fruition. I would like to first thank Kathleen Hackett for her expeditious editing and encouragement; writing recipes at 3 in the morning was bearable only because I knew she was often burning the digital midnight oil with me. Thank you to Chris Gaugler, whose design conveys beautifully the spirit of my cooking. Mitch Mandel took gorgeous photos with the assistance of the exceedingly helpful Troy Schnyder. A very big thank-you to food stylist Mariana Velasquez and her assistant Claudia Ficca for staying true to my recipes and making them look stunning. Stylist Hilary Robertson breathed life into every photo with the able assistance of Beth Flatley. Thank you all for a great experience. I'd also like to thank the Rodale team for the tremendous effort they displayed in seeing this book through: Elissa Altman, Anne Egan, Beth Lamb, Yelena Gitlin, and Hope Clarke.

I am deeply indebted to the crew of *MasterChef* USA Season 3, without whom none of this would exist. Thank you to all the casting coordinators and production assistants, especially Cara, Lynsey, Perry, Trask, Jen, Angie, Carter, Kayla, Tori, Sylvia, Sarina, CJ, Donny, Joel, Jeff, and JP. Your kinship was greatly appreciated during the time we were without. A heartfelt thanks to the culinary team—especially Sandee, Chef Jeff, Brad, Nicole, and Kevin—for your counsel, for the most beautiful pantry, and for cleaning up after us. Thank you to Brian, Anna, Will, and all those in direction; art and set construction; and hair, makeup, and wardrobe. I am grateful for the various producers—especially Robin, Adeline, Aaron, Yasmin, Adam, and Kim—for this amazing opportunity. Last but not least, I am indebted to Gordon, Graham, and Joe for their mentorship; thank you for believing in me before I believed in myself.

I'd also like to acknowledge the new family I've gained in the contestants of *MasterChef* Season 3, especially those in the cast of 18. I have learned so much from you, not just about food, but about life. Despite how different we all are, it is the love of cooking that bonds us. Thank you to Scott, Michael, Cowboy Mike, Frank, Stacey, Monti, Josh, D-Mar, Tali, D-Mack, Ryan, Anna, Helene, Samantha, Becky, Tanya, and Felix for sharing in this experience with me. I would like to thank Nancy for her dedication and late nights. I especially want to give my utmost gratitude to Cindy—you began as an extension of me, but by the end, you became a part of me.

I'd like to thank the following family and friends for their culinary advice, help, and inspiration: my cousin, Pauline; my neighbor, Tony; and my confidante, Sherry. Thank you to my Aunt Carol; Aunt Kim; and my mother-in-law, Yon, for filling the 20-year void in my life. And, of course, I am eternally grateful to my mother, who instilled in me integrity, perseverance, and curiosity.

I would also like to thank the staff at the Division for Blind Services, a part of the Department of Assistive and Rehabilitative Services of Texas, for helping me achieve a more independent life after my vision loss. They taught me to focus on my abilities instead of my disability, and the services and materials they provided are what made me the writer and chef I am today. A special thanks to Lori, Sharon, Ursula, Steve, Elaine, Anne, and Benigno for everything you've done for me.

Lastly, the moral support I received from a very dear handful of people is immeasurable. Thank you, Karen, for being my cheerleader and always reminding me that I shouldn't be afraid to dream big. You were the catalyst that helped me shed my fears and pursue my passions.

Thank you, Teresa, for your support in all areas, for holding my hand full circle from both auditions in Austin and L.A. to the finale reception in New York, and for your willingness to eat everything I cook. And, last but not least, I must thank you, John, for being my number one fan and toughest food critic—your candor makes me a stronger cook. Thank you for being both my pillar and my partner.

Index

Underscored page references indicate boxed text. **Boldfaced** page references indicate photographs.